VIRGINIA

REAL ESTATE SALESPERSON PRACTICE EXAMS AND STUDY GUIDE (STATE PORTION)

BY: THE REAL ESTATE TRAINING TEAM

IMPORTANT DISCLAIMERS

The information contained within this book is strictly for informational purposes. The author and publisher do no make any guarantee as to the accuracy of this work. The author does not assume and hereby disclaims any liability to any party for any loss, damage, or disruption caused by errors or omissions, whether such errors or omissions result from accident, negligence, or any other cause. We are not responsible for your actions and cannot guarantee results or success. The author of this book is not affiliated with PSI, DPOR or any of the Virginia State real estate boards. The use of the information in this book or any products and services recommended should be based on your own due diligence and you agree that our company is not liable for any success or failure in your business that is directly or indirectly related to the purchase and use of our information, products, or services.

TABLE OF CONTENTS

PREFACE

For additional real estate resources, training, videos, and much more, you can visit us online at www.therealestatetrainingteam.com.

HOW TO USE THIS BOOK

This book is intended to provide you with the knowledge necessary to pass the Virginia state portion of the real estate exam. Although you can skip directly to the practice exams, I would be sure to reference all of the material in this guide.

This guide first covers how the test works and what you need to know about taking the exam. Then there is a study guide page that includes the material in note form so that you can quickly reference the information. After that, we have five practice exams with answers. Then lastly, there is a real estate glossary of terms at the end to help you ace the exam.

The questions on these practice tests come directly from the Virginia state resources and a licensed Virginia real estate broker. There are 200 questions in this guide with five practice exams to give you a thorough understanding of the material. On the actual state Virginia Real Estate Exam, you will only get 40 questions.

While I can't guarantee you will pass the actual exam, I can say that if you spend just an afternoon on this material with focused study, your chances will significantly increase.

WHAT YOU NEED TO KNOW ABOUT THE TEST

1. What are the requirements for taking the test?

60 hours of studying from an approved provider; fingerprinting and ID; must be 18 and have a high school degree or equivalent.

2. How to register for an exam?

Once your education provider submits your required hours, you can register for your exam on www.psiexams.com, by calling them at 1-800-733-9267, or sending your application via mail to PSI.

3. How many questions does the Virginia Exam consist of?

40 questions.

4. How much time do you have to finish the exam?

45 minutes.

5. What is a passing score for the exam?

75%. In other words, you have to get at least 30 out of 40 questions correct.

6. What if you fail the first time?

You can re-take the exam as soon as the next day.

7. Where are the exam locations?

All over Virginia – for updated sites, look at PSI's website.

8. What do you need to bring on the day of the test?

You need two forms of ID, you have to arrive at least 30 minutes early, and there are storage bins for your things.

9. Additional info?

The exam is done mostly via computer and the test proctor will give you an introductory 15-minute tutorial on how to complete the exam.

10. When do you find out your score?

If you use a computer, the score will be given to you immediately following the exam completion. If you choose to take the test with paper and pencil, your results will be mailed to you.

QUICK STUDY GUIDE CHEAT SHEET

There are six different components to the test, and in this section, we will go over all the information in note form.

Part 1: Licensing

- Qualifications for a salesperson include: being at least 18 years old, having a high school diploma or equivalent, 60 hours of a qualifying real estate course, a reputation for honesty and fair dealing, no licenses from other areas that have been revoked, no convictions, no previous violations of fair housing laws.

- Qualifications for a broker: experience as a real estate salesperson for 36 of the past 48 months, being at least 21 years old, having 180 hours of approved real estate courses, a reputation for honesty and fair dealing, no previous convictions or violations.

- Who is exempt from real estate licensing requirements? This includes auctioneers, trustees, attorneys, and owners.

- License by reciprocity (reciprocal licenses): Virginia has licensee agreements with all states, meaning that if you have a license in another state, you can be licensed in Virginia with just a few requirements, including being in good standing.

- Broker's supervisory requirements include: a supervising broker at every branch office, providing adequate supervision and training to the licensees, conducting an audit of the brokerage at least every two years, maintaining records for three years and providing them upon request.

- Additional requirements for brokerages: must maintain a place of business in the Commonwealth of Virginia where real estate transactions can take place, must display the name of the brokerage, and make it clear that it is real estate including using words such as "real estate" or "realty."

- Virginia Real Estate Board: It has nine members, including seven licensed agents or brokers, two citizen members, and the terms of Board members is four years.

- Changes: The VREB (Virginia Real Estate Board) must be notified of changes in the brokerage address or name within 30 days. If a licensee is transferring to or from another brokerage, the VREB must be notified within ten days.

- VREB Authority: They can suspend or revoke licenses, deny a license renewal, put licensees on probation for further educational requirements, issue cease and desist orders to brokers, impose a civil penalty up to $2,500 per infraction, refer the matter to the commonwealth attorney, and they are not allowed to impose a prison sentence.

- DPOR (Virginia Department of Professional and Occupational Regulation) role: They enforce license and regulatory issues, handle complaints against licensees, and investigate unlicensed activities.

- Improper dealings include: when an agent does not disclose information to a client or customer, and they should have, not disclosing brokerage relationships, listing a property for sale on terms that the owner has not authorized.

- VREB requests: If VREB requests records or information, you have ten days to provide it to them.

- Conflicts of interest: If you receive compensation from someone other than your broker, then that is not allowed. You must also provide full disclosure and receive written permission of both parties to a transaction if you are representing more than one party in a deal.

- Misrepresentations and Omissions: This includes making false statements, untruthful advertising, or failing to disclose adverse facts.

- Improper brokerage: Acts include net listings (where a broker is allowed to keep the difference between the seller's listing price and the final sales price), paying a transaction-based fee to a non-licensed agent, accepting commissions from someone outside of the principal or supervising broker, commingling funds from an earnest money deposit.

- Virginia Real Estate Transaction Recovery Fund: New licensees must pay $20 into it; the fund must keep a minimum balance of $400,000; if the fund falls below the minimum balance, then each licensee will be assessed $20; the most amount a single claimant can recover from the fund is $20,000 for one transaction, if the fund exceeds 2 million; any excess money goes towards the Virginia Housing Partnership Fund; if a licensee is required to make a payment to the Transaction Recovery Fund then their license is automatically suspended.

- Brokerage audits: Principal or supervising brokers must audit their brokerage once every three years (or hire a professional to do so); if any noncompliance is found, they must notify the board within 30 days; the broker must either verify the noncompliance has been resolved or submit a plan to do so within 90 days. If the broker submits a successful audit report every three years, they will receive immunity from any enforcement actions from the board.

- Recordkeeping: Principal brokers must keep all records to a real estate deal for three years.

- Real estate education: Newly licensed agents are required to do 30 hours of post-licensing education within their first year of being licensed; if an agent has been licensed more than a year, the continuing education requirements are 16 hours every two years; brokers must complete 180 hours of study to apply for a broker's license and do 24 hours every two years for continuing education.

- Concurrent licenses: It is possible to be licensed at different brokerages at the same time so long as you have the written permission of both brokers and fill out the VREB form.

- Transferring a license: The steps to transfer a license include terminating your relationship with the current broker, completing a transfer application on Virginia's DPOR's website, having your new broker sign the form, and submitting the application to VREB.

Part 2: Disclosure Requirements

- Virginia Residential Property Disclosure Act: This requires that, whenever a property is for sale or lease (including for sale by owner and listing through a broker), there needs to be a property condition disclosure statement signed by the seller.

- New construction: In regard to home builders selling new construction, they don't have to fill out the disclosure form; however, they have to give written disclosure of any known building code violations.

- Caveat emptor: Virginia is a 'caveat emptor state,' which means "let the buyers beware." It means that the buyer should do all of their due diligence on a property and that the seller does not have to disclose all property information. However, a seller can't conceal any problems or lie in response to any questions about their property. An agent must also honestly disclose any information on material defects.

- Recourse for a buyer: If a buyer purchases a house with a defect (s), the buyer has to prove that the seller purposely covered up the defect or withheld information. Buyers have one year after closing to sue a seller for fraud if they believe the seller intentionally misled them.

- Exemptions from the Virginia Residential Property Disclosure Act: include court-ordered real estate sales, foreclosures, transfer among related parties, tax sales, and other associated sales.

- Property Disclosure Form Information: It is available on Virginia's DPOR (Department of Professional and Occupational Regulation) website. The form states that a buyer should do their due diligence and that it is the buyer's responsibility to find any defects. When no agents are involved, the seller must still fill out the form and give it to the buyer. Additionally, the form states that the seller makes no representation in regard to historic ordinances, whether or not the house is in the Chesapeake Bay Preservation Act area, sexual offenders in the area, and other specified information.

- Timeline for the Property Disclosure Form: The disclosure form needs to be provided by the seller before the contract is ratified, or the buyer can withdraw their offer without penalty. When the form is provided after going under contract, the buyer can cancel the sale within three days after the disclosure was delivered. The buyer is no longer able to cancel the sale after settlement if the disclosure was received after closing.

- Septic disclosure: Seller's don't have to disclose the presence of septic systems unless the current system is subject to repairs or maintenance, and the owner has been given a waiver for these requirements. The reason for this is that the waiver is not transferrable, and the new owner will have to bring the system up to the state board of health standards. When no septic disclosure is required, the seller should still do their due diligence on the septic system.

- Chesapeake Bay Act: This act was created to protect the Chesapeake Bay area, and sellers who are in this protected area may have development and zoning restrictions. However, sellers have no obligation to disclose this Act since it is the buyer's responsibility to find it out.

- Megan's Law: Megan's Law is a federal law where sex offenders are required to register in the state they live in. A seller does not have to disclose if any sex offenders live in the neighborhood; it is on the buyer to do their due diligence.

- Aircraft Noise Disclosure: If a seller is in an area that has been established as a noise zone, then they have to disclose that information to any buyer. The official zoning map has that information; however, if the noise zone is less than 65 average decibels, then this disclosure is not required.

- Stigmatized properties: These could include houses that have had felonies, homicides, suicides, been haunted, or had other issues that do not affect the physical structure of the property. Sellers and agents are not required to disclose this type of information.

- HIV/AIDS: It is a violation of federal law to disclose whether a previous seller or occupant had HIV or AIDS.

- Additional required disclosures: While Virginia is a 'buyer beware' state, there are several other disclosures a seller is required to make if they meet the criteria. These include defective drywall, pending building or zoning violations, septic systems that need maintenance and have a waiver, Planning District 15 (mining activities), military air installations (noise zones), whether or not the property was used to manufacture methamphetamines. However, if the property was used to manufacture meth and it was refurbished to meet state guidelines, then no disclosure is needed.

- Advertising requirements: The principal or managing broker is responsible for and must supervise all advertising by their agents. The agent and brokerage must have the written consent of the seller before advertising their property, and all for sale and for lease signs must have the firm name and office phone number. If the agent listing the property is also the owner, that must be disclosed. Business cards must have the agent's name, phone number, or website and have the brokerage's name. With online advertising, the main page must have the agent's name, brokerage name, and the city/state where they are located. If it's not the main page, then it should have this information or a link to it on the main page.

- HOA/POA disclosures: Homeowners Associations (HOAS) and Property Owners

Associations (POAs) must provide potential buyers with disclosure and resale packets from the community. The seller is responsible for providing the buyer with this information. The packets contain information such as budget, annual report, special assessments, rules and regulations, and more. An HOA/POA must deliver the packets within 14 days of the request, and buyers have three days from receiving or being told they are not available to cancel a contract without penalty.

Part 3: Escrow Accounts

- Requirements: Escrow accounts must be held in a federally insured account in Virginia. They don't have to bear interest, but if they do, then the broker must disclose in writing before entering a contract to all parties to the transaction. The account must be labeled as an 'escrow account.' The principal broker or supervising broker is responsible for the escrow account.

- What is escrow? These are accounts that hold the money for a buyer or seller in a transaction. Typically, this would include the earnest money deposit from a buyer, but it could also include down payment, security deposits, and settlement funds.

- Commingling: This is an illegal act whereby a broker would mix company or personal funds with the escrow funds.

- Conversion: This is an illegal act where a broker would use the money in an escrow account for something other than its purpose.

- Timeline for escrow: Earnest money must be deposited in an escrow account within five business days unless otherwise specified.

- Protecting Escrow Accounts: If the Virginia Real Estate Board (VREB) believes that the escrow funds are at risk, then they could appoint a receiver through the courts to handle the account.

- Disbursing escrow money: The principal broker disburses the money and only under these scenarios: a successful closing, a court order, or if all parties to the transaction agree to it in writing.

- Recordkeeping of escrow accounts: A broker must keep an accurate record of all escrow funds for three years.

Part 4: Agency Definitions and Relationships

- Brokerage agreements: These must be signed before performing any licensed real estate work for a client. Additionally, although the agent is performing the work, the agreement is between the firm and the client. All brokerage agreements must be in writing and describe the services offered, compensation, and any additional conditions.

- Brokerage disclosures: A licensee must disclose they work for a brokerage before having the first substantive discussion with a client about a property. If a broker is acting as a dual agent or designated agent, then they must get the written approval of all parties in the transaction.

- Standard agent duties: These include the following but are not limited to: perform per the terms of the brokerage agreement, help draft and negotiate offers and counteroffers, receive and present in a timely manner all offers and counteroffers, provide assistance to the client to help facilitate the settlement and more.

- Limited service agent: This is an agent who represents a client with typically fewer duties than a standard agent. There must be a limited-service agreement with the services that the agent will and will not provide.

- Documents: Agents must promptly deliver transaction documents, including offers and counteroffers to all parties in a transaction. They must also keep legible copies of all records from the transaction for at least three years.

- Duties to a client: A client is someone that the agent is representing, and the agent's duties include obedience, confidentiality, loyalty, disclosure, accounting, and reasonable skill and care.

- Duties to a customer: A customer is someone that the agent is not representing. An agent's duties include treating all parties honestly, informing the customer of their brokerage relationship with the other party, and disclosing any required deficiencies in the property.

- Misrepresentation: There are two types of misrepresentation, including intentional and unintentional misrepresentation. Intentional misrepresentation is when the agent knows something to be false, but they still say or write it anyways. Unintentional misrepresentation is when an agent makes a misstatement that harms a buyer. Although they were not trying to harm the buyer, they can be considered negligent because they should have known the statement was incorrect.

- Omission: This could include not presenting offers and counteroffers promptly, failing to disclose material facts about a property, and other scenarios that involve negligence.

- Designated agency: This is when a principal or supervising broker designates different agents within the same brokerage to work with the buyer and seller of the same transaction. Designated agency is typically less risky and more advantageous for both parties than a dual agency scenario where the same agent represents both sides of the deal. In designated agency, all parties must sign a disclosure acknowledgment form.

- Dual agency: This is when an agent represents both the buyer and seller in a transaction. Although it's illegal in many states, it is allowed in Virginia. To do a dual agency, the agent must get written disclosure of the consequences of dual agency and a written consent form to do dual agency.

- Unrepresented parties: If an agent is representing a client and the other party does not have an agent, they must disclose to the unrepresented party whom they represent. The agent is not allowed to give real estate advice to the unrepresented party, except for ministerial tasks such as filling in forms and related items.

- VREB Requests: If the Virginia Real Estate Board requests a record of any transaction the agent was involved in, they must produce it within ten days.

Part 5: Virginia Fair Housing Law and Regulations

- Who is protected: Protected classes in Virginia include race, color, national origin, sex, disability, familial status, religion, and the elderly (55 and up).

- Who is not protected: Non-protected classes in Virginia include drug dealers, students, smokers, unmarried couples, and gay or lesbian people.

- Exemptions to the fair housing laws: If a landlord owns three houses or fewer, and does not use a real estate agent or advertise in any way that the house is for sale or rent. Real estate agents are not allowed to violate the fair housing laws in any way, including the example mentioned above. Religious organizations are allowed to choose an applicant based on the same religion. Owners can do a background check on applicants and refuse an applicant based on previous criminal convictions.

- Submitting a complaint: To file a fair housing discrimination complaint, you must fill out and submit the housing discrimination form on DPOR's website. It must be filed within one year of the alleged fair housing discrimination act.

- Investigating a fair housing complaint: Once a fair housing discrimination complaint form is submitted, an investigator will review the issue, try to come to an agreement with the two parties, and publish a report that the Fair Housing Board and Real Estate Board will consider. If the two parties agree on a resolution, then the complaint will be dismissed, and if not, then the charge is referred to the attorney general's office for the next steps.

Part 6: Specific Acts Relating to Real Estate Practice

- Virginia Landlord and Tenant Act: The purpose of this act is to simplify and govern the laws and responsibilities of landlords and tenants.

- Tenants' responsibilities and rights: They must keep the property in a clean and safe condition, allow the landlord access within at least 24 hours' notice to make repairs or show the property, and completely vacate the property, including their belongings, at the end of the lease. If the landlord breaches the agreement, the tenant can serve notice for them to remedy the issue within 21 days, or they will vacate. If the landlord fails to provide basic services such as water and heat, then the tenant can recover reasonable damages. If a tenant who is a member of the armed forces receives a change order more than 35 miles away for more than three months, then they can terminate the lease without penalty.

- Landlord responsibilities and rights: They must disclose any mold, defective drywall, if the property was used to manufacture methamphetamine and noise zones. They must also comply with building and housing codes to keep the property safe and in working order. A landlord is not allowed to shut off water to a unit or refuse to allow a tenant to enter a unit.

- Virginia Time-Share Act Information: A buyer is allowed to cancel a contract without penalty within seven days after signing a contract. After receiving the certificate of resale for a time-share, a buyer has five days to cancel the contract.

- Virginia Condo Act Information: This act regulates how condos are created and sold. Condo developers must submit a declaration for each development, including the conditions and covenants of the development. Condo buyers have three days to cancel a contract once receiving the resale packet or being told it is not available.

- Virginia Underground Utility Prevention Act Information: This act was designed to protect consumers from utility lines, which may or may not be buried in a yard. Before doing any excavation or demolition, you are required to call 811. Once called, Miss Utility will come out and mark the underground utility lines to prevent any damage. If installing a for sale sign by hand or foot, then it is not necessary to call Miss Utility.

- Virginia Property Owners' Association Act Information: HOAs/POAs are created to enforce regulations for properties within their jurisdiction. HOAs/POAs are allowed to charge fees for maintenance, charge a special assessment for repairs if needed, and place liens on properties that don't pay their dues. The owners of properties in HOAs/POAs are allowed to access the HOA/POA financial records, vote on issues within the association, and be elected to the board of directors.

PRACTICE EXAM 1

1. What is the maximum payout for a single claimant from the transaction recovery fund?

a) $20,000

b) $100,000

c) $50,000

d) $10,000

2. What are the age requirements for getting a real estate license in Virginia?

a) 18

b) 21

c) 16

d) 25

3. What is the real estate board not allowed to do?

a) The board has the power to fine any licensee, as well as suspend or revoke a license.

b) The board can impose a prison sentence

c) The board establishes education requirements for licensure

d) The board may establish criteria outlining the permitted activities of unlicensed individuals employed by a real estate licensee

4. Salespersons who are not newly licensed are required to take how many hours of continuing education every year?

a) 24 hours

b) 30 hours

c) 16 hours

d) 8 hours

5. In regard to brokerage agreements, what is one requirement per the Virginia Real Estate Board regulations?

a) They can decide on the amount to be paid after going under contract.

b) They must be 6% for a listing agreement.

c) They can be verbal or written.

d) They must have a definite termination date.

6. How many years does it take to qualify for a broker's license?

a) 4 years, or at least 24 of the last 48 months of having been an actively engaged real estate salesperson

b) 3 years, or at least 36 of the last 48 months of having been an actively engaged real estate salesperson

c) 2 years, or at least 12 of the last 24 months of having been an actively engaged real estate salesperson

d) 5 years, or at least 48 of the last 60 months of having been an actively engaged real estate salesperson

7. At a brokerage, what must the Principal Broker do with the licenses of their agents?

a) The licenses need to be displayed, including the principal broker's license, as well the licenses of all the salespeople.

b) It is not necessary to display licenses at a brokerage office so long as there are available copies on file.

c) Only the principal broker's license needs to be displayed.

d) Only the salespeople's licenses need to be displayed since the principal broker is overseeing the office.

8. Within how many days must an earnest money deposit received by the broker be placed in an escrow account?

a) Within 5 business days unless otherwise agreed to in writing

b) Within 3 business days unless otherwise agreed to in writing

c) There is no time limit on placing an earnest money deposit in an escrow account.

d) Anytime, so long as it is before closing

9. How long must escrow records be kept?

a) At least 5 years from the settlement date

b) There is no time limit.

c) At least 3 years from the settlement date

d) They must be kept forever.

10. Is the broker required to hold earnest money deposits?

a) Yes, the listing broker is responsible for earnest money deposits in a transaction.

b) Yes, the broker is required to hold all earnest money deposits.

c) No, it is common and recommended for the title company to hold the earnest money deposit.

d) No, anyone can hold an earnest money deposit since the contract does not have to specify.

11. In the event that VREB believes escrow funds are at risk, what action can they take?

a) They can sue the buyer or seller to retrieve the funds.

b) They can petition the court to appoint a receiver to manage the escrow account.

c) They cannot take any action since the escrow fund are an issue between the brokers in the deal.

d) They can set up a mediation session.

12. All real estate advertising must have at least what items?

a) The firm's licensed name clearly and legibly displayed on all advertising.

b) Name, phone number, and website of the brokerage.

c) Website or phone number of the brokerage.

d) There are no requirements for real estate advertising.

13. All of the following are true in regard to 'caveat emptor,' except which one?

a) 'Caveat Emptor' means "let the buyer beware."

b) Virginia is a buyer beware state, which means the buyer should do all necessary due diligence.

c) A seller in Virginia does not have to disclose anything since it is a caveat emptor state.

d) The seller is not responsible for disclosing all defects; however, they also can't lie or actively conceal problems.

14. What would be the best way for a seller or buyer to find out if they are in a military aircraft noise zone?

a) They could look up the tax record in the county records.

b) They could ask the title company.

c) They could ask their real estate agent.

d) They could look up the area's official zoning map.

15. What are the repercussions if the buyer terminates the sale because the property disclosure was not provided?

a) There's no penalty so long as the buyer withdraws before settlement.

b) The buyer loses their earnest money deposit.

c) The buyer loses their earnest money deposit and potentially risks a further lawsuit from the seller for non-performance.

d) The buyer is not allowed to terminate a sale based on not receiving the property disclosure and will be in default.

16. What is Megan's Law?

a) A federal law that allows an individual who inhabits a neglected piece of real estate to claim ownership of the property after a certain amount of time

b) The right of a government to take ownership of private property for public use through just compensation

c) A federal law that requires sex offenders to register publicly with the state they live in

d) A federal law that makes it unlawful to discriminate against those with disabilities.

17. The Real Property Disclosure only applies to which of the following types of sales?

states any things wrong w/ the home. (doesn't matter w/ other answer options)

a) Transfers pursuant to court orders (bankruptcy, eminent domain, etc.)

b) Foreclosures

c) Listing a fixer-upper with a real estate agent that was just renovated

d) Transfers among co-owners

18. What are the cancellation timeframes for when a buyer receives HOA packets?

a) A buyer can cancel without penalty within 5 days of receiving the packet or within 5 days of being told that they are not available.

b) A buyer can cancel without penalty within 3 days of receiving the packet or within 3 days of being told that they are not available.

c) A buyer can cancel at any time before closing without penalty once receiving the HOA packet.

d) A buyer can cancel without penalty within 7 days of receiving the packet or within 7 days of being told that they are not available.

19. What type of agreement is needed for dual agency?

a) A verbal or written agreement is sufficient.

b) Written agreement from at least one of the parties in the transaction

c) Written agreement from the principal broker

d) Written consent of all parties to the transaction after having given written disclosure of the consequences of dual agency

20. Which of the statements below best describes how a limited-service agent works?

a) A verbal or written agreement that informs the client that they are only performing limited services in the real estate transaction.

b) If you market yourself as a limited-service agent, then no further disclosure is needed when working with clients.

c) A written agreement where the limited-service agent discloses they are acting as a limited-service agent and provides a list of the specific services that the licensee will and will not provide to the client.

d) This is where a friend or associate places your listing on the MLS for a small fee.

21. What does a common source information company do?

a) They compile information about real estate directly from the MLS and make it available to the public.

b) They provide data in regard to who in a neighborhood is most likely to be selling their property in the near future.

c) They track foreclosure notices and other public notices in a subscription format.

d) These are public companies that give an estimate about the value of a property based on their algorithm.

22. How does a concurrent license work?

a) When an agent has a license at two different brokerages, you need to have a concurrent license form and written verification from the principal brokers of each firm for this to be allowed.

b) A concurrent license is when you have your license active at two different brokerages.

c) When an agent has both a real estate license and an appraiser or home inspector license.

d) This is when an agent has a referral license and an active real estate license.

23. What would be an example of an intentional misrepresentation?

a) When the seller told a listing agent that the basement does not flood.

b) When a listing agent discloses information about a previous structural issue that has since been remediated.

c) When an agent relies on information from the public record about a property, and it turns out to be false.

d) When an agent or seller lies or conceals information about a property. It is similar to fraud.

24. When is the disclosure of agency form required?

a) This form is only required in the state of Virginia and must be given before writing a contract to buy or sell a property.

b) This form must be given in writing or verbally as early as practical upon having a substantive discussion about a specific property in a real estate transaction.

c) It must be given at any time before closing to the buyer or seller.

d) It must be made in writing as early as practical upon having a substantive discussion about a specific property in a real estate transaction.

25. What are the different ways an agent can represent a client in Virginia?

a) Limited service agent, standard agent, independent contractor

b) Principal broker, managing broker, associate broker

c) Referral agent, real estate licensee, real estate broker

d) Client, principal, customer

26. When someone just wants their property listed on the MLS and doesn't need or want much assistance, what is the person they work with known as?

a) Full-service agent

b) Independent contractor

c) Limited service agent

d) Principal broker

27. What statutory duties does an agent owe their client?

a) The duties of finding a great real estate deal, duty of negotiation, duty of deal analysis

b) The duties of acting in the best interests of the client, duty of confidentiality, duty of exercising reasonable care

c) The duties of accounting, duty of real estate brokerage, duty of staging

d) The duties of disclosure, duty of financing, duty of trusted referrals

28. For what type of real estate transactions is a written brokerage agreement required?

a) Only on a listing

b) It is always required before performing any licensed activities, including showing a house or listing a property on the MLS.

c) Only on the purchase of a property

d) Only if the seller or buyer requests a written agreement

29. What happens if an agent gets an offer that's way under market value and the seller already has another offer?

a) An agent has to present any offers no matter how low or even if the property is already under contract.

b) Agents only have to present offers if the property is not yet under contract

c) Since agents represent the seller, they can choose which offer to present to the seller and can exclude certain offers.

d) If the offer is at least 10% lower than the asking price, the agent is not required to present the offer to the seller.

30. What is considered a mental disability according to the Virginia Fair Housing Board?

a) Drug addiction

b) Alcoholism

c) Chronic hoarding

d) ADD

31. How long do people accused of violating the Fair Housing Law have to be notified of their complaint against them and their rights?

a) 7 days

b) 3 days

c) 30 days

d) 10 days

32. Who is exempt from fair housing laws?

a) A real estate agent who is listing their personal property

b) A landlord that owns no more than three homes and does not use a real estate agent or advertise the property

c) Any landlord that is not licensed

d) A home inspector and appraiser

33. Can an over-55 community exclude kids?

a) It depends

b) Yes

c) No, that would be a fair housing violation

d) All of the above, since each community is different.

34. With condos in Virginia, how are votes on the condo board typically determined?

a) In proportion to square feet

b) By purchase price of the condo

c) By the number of bedrooms

d) By an election in the condo association

35. How many days does a buyer have to withdraw their offer without penalty after they get a resale certificate from an owner on a condo?

a) 5 days to review

b) 3 days to review and rescind the contract, the same amount of time as an HOA

c) 7 days to review

d) Any time before closing

36. Virginia underground utility damage prevention act. What is the phone number to call before excavating or doing any construction?

a) Call the local gas company.

b) Call a local plumber to verify the excavating is okay.

c) Call the county to verify.

d) 811, also known as Miss Utility.

37. What is one of the tenants' basic duties under the VA residential landlord and tenant act?

a) Hire a weekly cleaning company.

b) They must allow access at any time to the landlord to check on the property.

c) They must keep two months' worth of rent in an escrow account for any necessary repairs.

d) They must keep the property in a clean and safe condition.

38. What happens when a rental property is sold?

a) The lease is canceled, and the tenant must leave.

b) The lease is continued but must be re-negotiated before closing.

c) The lease continues.

d) The tenant will automatically be on a month-to-month tenancy.

39. What would be an example of a conflict of interest?

a) Representing more than one client in a transaction without first getting the written consent of all clients in the transaction.

b) Negotiating for a client by starting significantly under the price they would pay for a property.

c) Telling a potential buyer that there are no structural issues with a house when, in fact, you are aware of structural problems.

d) Listing a property for a client without providing any services other than placing their property on the MLS.

40. What best describes a licensee who does not list, buy, or sell property?

a) Associate broker

b) Referral agent

c) Principal broker

d) Appraiser

ANSWER KEY TO EXAM 1

1. A, $20,000

2. A, 18

3. B, The board can impose a prison sentence

4. C, 16 hours

5. D, They must have a definite termination date.

6. B, 3 years, or at least 36 of the last 48 months of having been an actively engaged real estate salesperson.

7. A, The licenses need to be displayed, including the principal broker's license, as well as the licenses of all the salespeople.

8. A, Within 5 business days, unless otherwise agreed to in writing.

9. C, At least 3 years from the settlement date

10. C, No, in fact, it is common and recommended for the title company to hold the earnest money deposit.

11. B, They can petition the court to appoint a receiver to manage the escrow account.

12. A, The firm's licensed name clearly and legibly displayed on all advertising

13. C, A seller in Virginia does not have to disclose anything since it is a caveat emptor state.

14. D, They could look up the area's official zoning map.

15. A, There's no penalty so long as the buyer withdraws before settlement.

16. C, Federal law that requires sex offenders to register publicly with the state they live in

17. C, Listing a fixer-upper that was just renovated with a real estate agent

18. B, A buyer can cancel without penalty within 3 days of receiving the packet or within 3 days of being told that they are not available.

19. D, Written consent of all parties to the transaction after having given written disclosure of the consequences of dual agency.

20. C, A written agreement where the limited-service agent discloses they are acting as a limited-service agent and provides a list of the specific services that the licensee will and will not provide to the client.

21. A, It compiles information about real estate directly from the MLS and makes it available to the public.

22. B, A concurrent license is when you have your license active at two different brokerages.

23. D, When an agent or seller lies or conceals information about a property. It is similar to fraud.

24. D, It must be made in writing as early as practical, upon having a substantive discussion about a specific property or properties in a residential real estate transaction

25. A, Limited service agent, standard agent, independent contractor

26. C, Limited service agent

27. B, The duties of acting in the best interests of the client, duty of confidentiality, duty of exercising reasonable care

28. B, It is always required before performing any licensed activities, including showing a house or listing a property on the MLS.

29. A, An agent has to present any offers no matter how low or even if the property is already under contract.

30. C, Chronic hoarding

31. D, 10 days

32. B, A landlord that owns no more than three homes and does not use a real estate agent or advertise the property

33. B, Yes

34. A, In proportion to square feet

35. B, 3 days to review and rescind the contract, the same amount of time as an HOA

36. D, 811, also known as Miss Utility

37. D, Keep the property in a clean and safe condition.

38. C, The lease continues.

39. A, Representing more than one client in a transaction without first getting the written consent of all clients in the transaction.

40. B, Referral agent

PRACTICE EXAM 2

1. What is the minimum balance the Transaction Recovery fund must keep?

    a) $400,000

    b) $100,000

    c) $250,000

    d) $300,000

2. What happens to an agent who makes a payment to the fund as a result of improper or dishonest conduct?

    a) The agent is banned for 3 years from being licensed in the state of Virginia.

    b) The agent's license is suspended 1 year, and they have to pay the full amount of the claim.

    c) Upon payment, the board shall immediately revoke the license of the agent and will not be eligible to apply until the payment has been repaid.

    d) The agent just has to pay the amount of the claim.

3. What type of real estate professional is a real estate firm required to have?

    a) Associate broker

b) Real estate salesperson

c) Fiduciary

d) Principal broker

4. What is a requirement if you have a license suspended or revoked in another jurisdiction?

a) You must notify the Virginia Real Estate Board.

b) There are no requirements since real estate laws are different from state to state.

c) You must take additional continuing education classes.

d) You must take additional continuing education classes and wait at least one year before getting a license.

5. What would be an example of intentional misrepresentation in a real estate deal?

a) Signing a limited-service agent agreement with your client.

b) Offering a property for sale or rent with the intent to sell it at a different price than advertised.

c) Negotiating with the seller by offering a low-ball first offer, knowing your client can come up in price.

d) Not signing a brokerage agreement with your client.

6. What is the process for changing brokerages?

a) Bring the physical copy of your old license over to your new brokerage.

b) Return your license to the board and re-take the exam to qualify for the brokerage.

c) Let your current broker know and file a request to transfer form with VREB that has signatures from both your old and new broker.

d) Email DPOR, and they will send an updated license copy within three business days.

7. What type of account must a broker escrow account be held in?

a) A federally insured depository in Virginia

b) Brokerage firm

c) Insurance company

d) CPA firm

8. If a property is not going to closing, and neither side of the transaction is willing to sign a release of the earnest money deposit, a broker may send notice that the funds will be released unless a written response is received from the principal who is not getting the funds within how many days?

a) 30 days

b) 15 days

c) 7 days

d) 10 days

9. What is conversion?

a) This is a report on similar homes in the area to determine the value of the subject property.

b) This is the schedule of your mortgage payments over the period of your loan.

c) This is when a seller lists a property without the help of a real estate agent to avoid paying commission fees.

d) Using funds from an escrow account to pay for other expenses that are not related.

10. What is required in the labeling of escrow accounts?

a) All escrow accounts shall be labeled 'escrow.'

b) The buyer can designate what they would like to label the escrow account.

c) The escrow account can be labeled 'escrow' account or 'earnest money' account.

d) There are no requirements of labeling escrow accounts, except to keep reasonable care and handling of the funds.

11. What is one type of seller disclosure not required in Virginia?

a) If the seller has a septic system that needs repair and the seller has a waiver from the State Board of Health.

b) If the seller has pending building/zoning violations.

c) If the seller's house is located in the Chesapeake Bay preservation area.

d) If the seller's home is located in a military noise/crash area.

12. If a listing agent relies on information from their client and public record on a property they are listing, can they be held liable for misrepresentation if the information turns out to be false?

a) No

b) Yes

c) Depends

d) A and C

13. How many units does the Real Property Disclosure apply to?

a) Any property under 10 units

b) Any type of real estate

c) Single-family homes only

d) Properties with 1 to 4 units

14. What is the listing agent's responsibility in regard to Megan's law?

a) The listing agent has no obligation to research or disclose sexual offenders in the vicinity.

b) The listing agent must look up the Megan's law sexual offender database and disclose relevant information on sexual offenders.

c) The listing agent only has to disclose Megan's Law offenders if a buyer or buyer's agent asks about it.

d) If the listing agent knows of any Megan's law offenders in the neighborhood, they must always disclose that information.

15. What are the drywall disclosure requirements in Virginia?

a) If the owner has knowledge of defective drywall, they must provide a written disclosure to the prospective buyer.

b) There are no disclosure requirements in regard to drywall.

c) Even if the owner is aware of defective drywall, Virginia is a buyer beware state, so they don't have to provide that information.

d) Defective drywall is not a structural issue, so no disclosure is required.

16. Do sellers need to mention the Chesapeake Preservation Act if their property is located in this affected area?

a) Yes, the seller must disclose any type of preservation areas they are in

b) Yes, since it affects the property value, a seller must disclose this information.

c) No, they don't need to mention it unless asked about it. It is the buyer's responsibility to discover that.

d) No, since Virginia is a buyer beware state, sellers do not need to disclose any information about the property.

17. If a seller is selling a property in an HOA/POA community, then what do they need to do?

a) Sellers should provide a resale and disclosure packet to a buyer to help them be more informed on the purchase.

b) Sellers must provide a resale and disclosure packet to a buyer, or the buyer can withdraw their offer.

c) An HOA or POA packet is nice to have but not necessary.

d) The buyer must purchase the HOA/POA packet and do all necessary due diligence on the HOA.

18. What is a requirement of advertising a property?

a) There must be a real estate sign visible at the property that is for sale or for rent.

b) An agent and company must have the written consent of the seller or landlord.

c) The property must be input in the MLS.

d) The commission must be 6% if the property is being listed for sale.

19. What happens when a brokerage is audited, and there were several items of noncompliance found?

a) The principal broker must fix the issue(s) and submit a statement acknowledging it has been remediated or put in a plan to correct the non-compliance within 90 days.

b) The principal broker is fined and put on suspension until the issues have been resolved.

c) The offending agents will automatically have their licenses suspended for 30 days and must resolve the issue.

d) The broker has 30 days to resolve the issue, or they will be fined up to $2,000 for each infraction.

20. To whom must listing agents disclose in writing their agency status to?

a) To the title company

b) To a buyer or seller at any time before closing

c) To a buyer at any time before the buyer submits an offer

d) An unrepresented buyer upon having a substantive discussion about real estate

21. What is an associate broker?

a) The broker that manages a real estate office or real estate team

b) A broker who is not the principal broker but is a licensed agent

c) A broker who also shares property management duties for different agents

d) A newly licensed agent

22. Who is not protected under the fair housing law?

a) Elderly people

b) People with a disability

c) Students

d) Chronic hoarders

23. All of these are an example of unlawful discrimination, except what?

a) Refusing to show a rental property to a family because they have several kids and the landlord would prefer no kids
b) A woman in a two-bedroom condo who only advertises for another woman to live with
c) A real estate agent who refuses to work with anyone outside of their race
d) A property manager who advertises for a 'Christian only' tenant

24. When advertising for a roommate, which of the following criteria are you not allowed to advertise for?

a) Religion
b) Gender
c) Smoking
d) Drinking

25. Which of the following best describes the Common Interest Community Board?

a) They are responsible for regulating the licensure and certification of common interest community (HOA) management firms and their employees. They also establish training and education requirements.

b) They protect the public interest against fraud, misrepresentation, dishonesty, and incompetence in real estate transactions.

c) They provide continuing and post-licensing education classes to realtors nationwide.

d) They are a part of DPOR and regulate who is allowed to obtain a real estate license.

26. What is the process for changing a rental agreement?

a) Landlord and tenant have to agree in writing to any changes.

b) You can't change a rental agreement once it has been signed.

c) The landlord can unilaterally change a rental agreement so long as they give 30 days' notice.

d) The tenant can request a change, and so long as it is under $250 in value, it has to be approved.

27. Why do you need to call 811 before installing a real estate sign in a yard?

a) To make sure that you get the correct permit

b) So that you can have a qualified contractor do the installation

c) So that the county can warn you if there are any gas lines in the yard

d) So that the utility lines beneath the ground can be marked with flags

28. How much notice must a landlord give a tenant to enter an apartment for a non-emergency?

a) 7 days' notice

b) At least 24 hours' notice

c) 3 days' notice

d) 10 days' notice

29. All of the following is true about a public offering statement by a condo developer, except what?

a) All purchasers of a condo must be given the public offering statement and it must be given at the time of entering into a contract for the purchase.

b) It is not intended to be all-inclusive, and the purchaser should still do their due diligence.

c) A purchaser has 5 days to review the public offering statement and withdraw for any reason without penalty.

d) The public offering statement shows comparable recent sales to justify their offering price.

30. How many days does a buyer have to review the public offering statement and rescind the contract?

a)   5 days
b)   7 days
c)   24 hours
d)   10 days

31. What would be an example of an improper brokerage commission?

a)   Another agent giving the principal broker a bonus for an agent doing a great job on a transaction.

b)   A seller giving the listing agent a bonus for doing a great job without the bonus going through the principal broker first.

c)   A listing agent paying a buyer's agent outside of closing for having a smooth transaction.

d)   A buyer's agent paying a home inspector a bonus for not disclosing information that would cause the buyer to back out.

32. What tenant rights do armed forces and National Guard members have under the Virginia residential landlord and tenant act?

a)   They can break the lease without penalty if they receive change orders of more than 35 miles away from the property or if they are discharged.

b) They have the same rights as any other tenant would have.

c) They are allowed to break their lease without penalty if they decide they want to.

d) They must pay a one-month rent payment if they choose to break their lease.

33. What is the primary purpose of the Virginia Property Disclosure form?

a) It warns buyers that the sellers are not responsible for disclosing many property defects and that the buyer should do their due diligence.

b) To have sellers disclose and list out all of the issues or potential issues with their property.

c) It gives the buyer a brief history of the property from the sellers' point of view.

d) It is a form the lender requires to make sure the property is in livable condition.

34. All of the following are included in an HOA/POA disclosure and resale certificate, except for what?

a) The current amount of reserve funds

b) The HOA/POA rules and regulations

c) Recent comparable sales in the community

d) Minutes from the all condo board or HOA meetings

35. If a licensed agent is representing a buyer in a transaction, then what duties do they have to the seller?

a) Honesty

b) Disclosure in regard to whether this will be a principal residence

c) Disclosure in regard to brokerage relationships

d) All of the above

36. Duties to a customer include all of the following, except for what?

a) Honesty

b) Loyalty

c) Disclosure

d) Accounting

37. After signing a contract, how many days does a purchaser of a time-share have to cancel the contract without penalty in Virginia?

a) 7 days

b) 5 days

c) 10 days

d) 3 days

38. What are some examples of what DPOR investigates?

a) Real estate investment companies
b) Predatory lenders
c) Off-market regulatory violations, unlicensed agent activity
d) Real estate joint ventures

39. What kind of real estate license from another state can be accepted in Virginia with the proper paperwork?

a) Concurrent license
b) Reciprocal license
c) Broker's license
d) Referral license

40. How do you file a fair housing complaint?

a) Call the National Association of Realtors and talk to a fair housing representative.
b) Talk with the principal broker of the brokerage where the alleged incident occurred.
c) Talk to a fair housing lawyer to properly file the complaint.
d) Fill out a form on DPOR's website.

ANSWER KEY TO EXAM 2

1. A, $400,00

2. C, Upon payment, the board shall immediately revoke the license of the agent and will not be eligible to apply until the payment has been repaid.

3. D, A principal broker

4. A, You must notify the Virginia Real Estate Board.

5. B, Offering a property for sale or rent with the intent to sell it a different price than advertised

6. C, Let your current broker know and file a request to transfer form with VREB that has signatures from both your old broker and new broker.

7. A, A federally insured depository in Virginia

8. B, 15 days

9. D, Using funds from an escrow account to pay for other expenses that are not related

10. A, All escrow accounts shall be labeled 'escrow'

11. C, If the seller's house is located in the Chesapeake Bay preservation area

12. A, No

13. D, properties with 1 to 4 units

14. A, The listing agent has no obligation to research or disclose sexual offenders in the vicinity.

15. A, If the owner has knowledge of defective drywall, they must provide a written disclosure to the prospective buyer.

16. C, No, they don't need to mention it unless asked about it. It is the buyer's responsibility to discover that.

17. B, Sellers must provide a resale and disclosure packet to a buyer.

18. B, An agent and company must have the written consent of the seller or landlord.

19. A, The principal broker must fix the issue(s) and submit a statement acknowledging it has been remediated or put in a plan to correct the non-compliance within 90 days.

20. D, An unrepresented buyer at the time of a substantive discussion about real estate

21. B, A broker who is not the principal broker but is a licensed agent

22. C, Students

23. B, A woman in a two-bedroom condo who only advertises for another woman to live with

24. B, Gender

25. A, They are responsible for regulating the licensure and certification of common interest community (HOA) management firms and their employees. They also establish training and education requirements.

26. A, Landlord and tenant have to agree in writing to any changes.

27. D, So that the utility lines beneath the ground can be marked with flags

28. B, At least 24 hours' notice

29. D, The public offering statement shows comparable recent sales to justify their offering price.

30. A, 5 days

31. B, A seller giving the listing agent a bonus for doing a great job without the bonus going through the principal broker first.

32. A, They can break the lease without penalty if they receive change orders of more than 35 miles away from the property or if they are discharged.

33. A, It warns the buyer's that the sellers are not responsible for disclosing many property defects and that the buyer should do their due diligence.

34. C, Recent comparable sales in the community

35. D, All of the above

36. B, Loyalty – this is a duty to a client

37. A, 7 days

38. C, Regulatory violations, unlicensed agent activity

39. B, Reciprocal license

40. D, Fill out a form on DPOR's website.

PRACTICE EXAM 3

1. How much must each new licensee pay to the transaction recovery fund?

    a) $20

    b) $40

    c) $100

    d) $50

2. Whom is the real estate board composed of?

    a) 10 members, including 5 real estate brokers with at least 5 years of experience and 5 real estate salespersons

    b) 7 members, including 3 real estate brokers, 2 real estate agents, and 2 citizen members

    c) 12 members, including 8 real estate brokers or agents with at least 5 years of experience and 4 citizen members

    d) 9 members, 7 who have been licensed agents or brokers for at least 5 consecutive years and 2 citizen members.

3. The following are allowed to be a settlement agent in Virginia, except who?

    a) A licensed title company

    b) A licensed attorney

c) A real estate salesperson

d) A real estate broker

4. What are the different CE requirements for agents and brokers?

a) Brokers have 24 hours of CE every licensing term. Salespersons have 16 hours every licensing term.

b) Brokers have 12 hours of CE every licensing term, while salespersons have 24 hours.

c) Brokers have 36 hours of CE every licensing term, while salespersons have 24.

d) Brokers have 40 hours of CE every licensing term, while salespersons have 36.

5. In how many days does a principal broker have to return an agent's license to the VREB if they are transferring brokerages?

a) 7 days

b) 10 days

c) 30 days

d) 14 days

6. What are the required education hours to apply for a broker's license?

a) 180 hours of board-approved courses

b) 80 hours of board-approved courses

c) 60 hours of board-approved courses

d) 50 hours of board-approved courses

7. Which of the following is an acceptable form of payment for an escrow account?

a) Jewelry

b) Promissory note

c) Check

d) Car title

8. What happens to the earnest money deposit at settlement?

a) The buyer gets refunded the amount at closing in the form of a check or wire.

b) The buyer and seller split the amount of the earnest money deposit.

c) The buyer, seller, and real estate agents split the amount evenly at closing.

d) It goes towards the buyer's closings costs and purchase of the home.

9. What is the minimum amount for an earnest money deposit?

a) No minimum, so long as both parties agree in writing

b) $500

c) 1% of the contract price

d) 3% of the contract price

10. Can property managers use money in escrow for repairs?

a) Yes, the money is there for that purpose

b) No, unless there is an agreement in writing from the owner.

c) Depends on the situation.

d) So long as the money is put back within 7 days, then yes.

11. When must the residential property disclosure be delivered to the buyer?

a) Prior to the contract being accepted

b) At any time before closing

c) Only when the buyer requests a copy

d) At the settlement table

12. What does Virginia law require a builder to disclose about a property?

a) Any known material defects that would be a violation of building code

b) If the property is in the Chesapeake Bay protection area

c) A certification of the type of drywall used in construction

d) If the builder has had any violations on construction projects in the past 3 years

13. When is a septic system written disclosure required?

a) If there is a septic system on the property, it must be disclosed.

b) A septic disclosure is never required since this is a buyer beware state.

c) If a septic system requires additional repairs by the Board of Health and the owner has a waiver

d) If the septic system is more than 10 years old, it must be disclosed.

14. If the seller is not required to make any disclosure about their septic system, then what is true?

a) The system must be in working order, and there is no need for an inspection.

b) It is recommended that the buyer still do their due diligence and inspection of the system

c) Their septic system has a 3-year warranty, and no disclosure is necessary.

d) Certain counties in Virginia do not require any septic disclosure, and it's best to check in your specific area.

15. What is true in regard to a buyer or seller inquiring about someone having AIDS or HIV in a house?

a) It is illegal to reveal someone's HIV or AIDS status if someone asks you.

b) A seller must disclose this information, but only if they are directly asked about it.

c) It must be disclosed on the property disclosure form.

d) An agent can decide whether or not to disclose that information at their discretion.

16. What best describes the definition of advertising in Virginia?

a) Passing out real estate business cards at a networking event

b) Running Facebook ads to your real estate company

c) Telling friends and family to refer others to your services

d) Any form of representation, promotion, or solicitation related to licensed real estate activity

17. How long are the implied warranties for structural defects in new construction properties?

a) 1 year ?
b) 2 years
c) 3 years
d) No time limit on structural defects

18. How many days does a homeowner's association (HOA) have to deliver the association disclosure packet once the seller has requested it?

a) 7 days maximum
b) 10 days maximum
c) 21 days maximum
d) 14 days maximum

19. How long must an agent and broker maintain their real estate records of previous deals?

a) 5 years
b) 1 year
c) 3 years
d) 7 years

20. At what time must an agent enter into a brokerage agreement with their buyer client?

a) Before giving substantive real estate advice about a property.

b) Any time before closing is sufficient.

c) Buyer clients don't require a brokerage agreement; only listing a property requires an agreement.

d) Within 30 days of talking with their client about the latter's real estate needs.

21. What types of real estate relationships do not have full duties under the Virginia real estate agency law?

a) Standard agent and associate broker

b) Limited service and independent contractor

c) Principal broker and independent contractor

d) Licensee and a standard agent

22. How long must a listing agent keep a property disclosure form?

a) 3 years

b) 5 years

c) 1 year

d) No time limit required for a disclosure form

23. What must be included in a brokerage agreement?

a) The appraisal of the property

b) The qualification letter from the lender for each client to ensure they are qualified financially

c) The terms and conditions of what brokerage services will be included

d) At least 3 recommendations from previous clients or other real estate professionals

24. How many days does a licensee have to produce a record of a real estate transaction in which the licensee was involved?

a) 7 business days

b) 30 days

c) 5 business days

d) 10 days if VREB requests it

25. What are the age requirements to meet the fair housing protected class of elderliness in Virginia?

a) 55

b) 60

c) 65

d) 50

26. **How many days to let the real estate board know about a change in name or address as a licensee?**

    a)   10 days

    b)   14 days

    c)   7 days

    d)   30 days

27. **How long does someone have to submit a fair housing complaint?**

    a)   There is no time frame.

    b)   It has to be filed within one year of the alleged discrimination.

    c)   Any complaint must be filed within 6 months.

    d)   There are 3 years within which a complaint can be filed.

28. **What is a landlord's responsibility when renting their property to (a) tenant(s)?**

    a)   The owner must comply with housing codes that could affect the health and safety of the tenant.

    b)   The landlord must rent the property at a price within 25% of the current market rate.

    c)   The landlord must provide the tenant with a phone number for maintenance items.

d) The landlord is only allowed to stop by the property once a month to check on the condition.

29. How much can a security deposit be for a tenant?

a) It can't be more than one month.

b) There is no limit so long as both parties agree in writing.

c) It can't be more than 2 months.

d) It can't be more than 3 months.

30. How many days does a landlord have to refund the rental application deposit if the applicant fails to rent the unit?

a) 20 days

b) 14 days

c) 30 days

d) 7 days

31. What must occur if a tenant pays their rent in cash?

a) No further action is needed, since the rent is paid.

b) Since the tenant paid in cash, they will not receive a copy of the rent being paid.

c) Only check, money order, or wire are acceptable forms of payment for rent.

d) The landlord has to give the tenant a receipt of payment upon request from the tenant.

32. What is one of the responsibilities of a principal or managing broker?

a) Planning out marketing campaigns for their agents

b) Reviewing their agents' work and providing training opportunities

c) Handling the accounting for each agent

d) Showing properties and attending home inspections when needed on behalf of their agents

33. Duties required of a standard agent include all of the following except for what?

a) They must perform their duties in accordance with the signed brokerage agreement.

b) They must help to write and negotiate offers and counteroffers.

c) They must disclose all the known material facts about a property to their buyer.

d) They must present the buyer with off-market properties that are not listed with an agent.

34. If a homeowner in an HOA/POA does not pay their dues, then what is the most likely scenario?

a) The HOA can place a lien on the property for the amount owed.

b) The HOA fee will automatically be added to the tax bill at the end of the year.

c) The HOA can sue the homeowner.

d) The HOA will go bankrupt.

35. The continuing education requirements for salespersons include all of the following topics, except which one?

a) Ethics

b) Fair housing

c) Contracts

d) How to market for off-market real estate listings

36. All of the following are allowed under Virginia Fair housing law, except what?

a) Denying a rental to someone because they have previous drug-dealing convictions

b) Denying a rental to someone because their credit is awful

c) Denying a rental to someone because they have kids

d) Denying a rental to someone because there would be too many occupants in the property

37. Duties owed to a client include all of the following, except what?

a) Obedience
b) Loyalty
c) Confidentiality
d) Ministerial duties

38. Where can you get access to the seller disclosure form for Virginia?

a) Only licensed realtors can access this form through their MLS.
b) On Virginia's Department of Professional and Occupational Regulation (DPOR) website.
c) It is available for purchase on the National Association of Realtor's Website for each state.
d) A seller must request the form through a licensed real estate broker.

39. How often is a principal or supervising broker required to audit their brokerage?

a) Every 3 years
b) Every year
c) Every other year

d)   Every 5 years

40. All of the following are not required to have a real estate license, except whom?

a)   Power of attorney sale
b)   Auctioneer selling real estate for an owner
c)   An agent listing their residence on the MLS
d)   Persons selling under the judgment of a court order

ANSWER KEY TO EXAM 3

1. A, $20

2. D, 9 members, 7 who have been licensed agents or brokers for at least 5 consecutive years and 2 citizen members

3. C, A real estate salesperson

4. A, Brokers have 24 hours of CE every licensing term. Salespersons have 16 hours every licensing term.

5. B, 10 days

6. A, 180 hours of board-approved courses

7. C, Check

8. D, It goes towards the buyer's closings costs and purchase of the home.

9. A, No minimum so long as both parties agree in writing

10. B, No, unless there is an agreement in writing from the owner.

11. A, Prior to the contract being accepted.

12. A, Any known material defects that would be a violation of building code

13. C, If a septic system requires additional repairs by the Board of Health and the owner has a waiver.

14. B, It is recommended that the buyer still do their due diligence and inspection of the system.

15. A, It is illegal to reveal someone's HIV or AIDS status if someone asks you.

16. D, Any form of representation, promotion, or solicitation related to licensed real estate activity

17. A, 1 year

18. D, 14 days maximum

19. C, 3 years

20. A, Before giving substantive real estate advice about a property

21. B, Limited service and independent contractor

22. A, 3 years

23. C, The terms and conditions of what brokerage services will be included

24. D, 10 days if VREB requests it

25. A, 55

26. D, 30 days

27. B, It has to be filed within one year of the alleged discrimination.

28. A, The owner must comply with housing codes that could affect the health and safety of the tenant.

29. C, It can't be more than 2 months.

30. A, 20 days

31. D, The landlord has to give the tenant a receipt of payment upon request from the tenant.

32. B, Reviewing their agents' work and providing training opportunities

33. D, They must present the buyer with off-market properties that are not listed with an agent.

34. A, The HOA can place a lien on the property for the amount owed.

35. D, How to market for off-market real estate listings

36. C, Denying a rental to someone because they have kids

37. D, Ministerial duties

38. B, On Virginia's Department of Professional and Occupational Regulation (DPOR) website

39. A, Every 3 years

40. C, An agent listing their residence on the MLS

PRACTICE EXAM 4

1. What is one of the items that the timeshare community books and records must have?

   a) An up-to-date list of all the timeshare owners in that community

   b) The recent sales in the community

   c) A recommended list of vendors for property maintenance

   d) A brief history of the timeshare development

2. How much time does a landlord have to make a final inspection after the end of a lease?

   a) 7 days

   b) 72 hours

   c) 48 hours

   d) 30 days

3. What is the maximum charge for an HOA packet?

   a) $50 for a hard copy, $50 for an electronic copy.

   b) HOAs are not allowed to charge for an HOA packet.

   c) There is no maximum; each HOA determines it.

d) $150 for a hard copy, $125 for an electronic copy.

4. The responsibilities of POAs or property owner's associations' include all of the following, except what?

a) Charging fees for maintenance of common areas

b) Placing liens on properties if the homeowner does not pay their dues

c) Making and voting on rules for properties within their association

d) Taking a property through eminent domain to create a public park or area

5. Whom must developers register their condo documents with?

a) DPOR

b) Virginia Fair Housing Office

c) Virginia Common Interest Community Board

d) National Association of Realtors

6. What is allowed in Virginia Fair Housing Law?

a) You are allowed to refuse a rental to a felon so long as all the potential tenants were treated the same way.

b) Advertising for a Christian roommate

c) Advertising a property for rent at double what the market rent currently is

d) Refusing to rent to someone with kids

7. Which organization enforces fair housing law for real estate agents?

a) It is investigated by the Virginia Fair Housing Office; however, the VREB will discipline licensees for violations.

b) National Association of Realtors

c) The Real Estate Commission

d) DPOR

8. Which of the following best describes dual agency?

a) This is when one agent represents both the buyer and seller in the same transaction.

b) This is when you have a real estate license at multiple brokerages.

c) This is when two agents from the same company are representing a buyer and seller in a transaction.

d) This is when a licensed real estate agent is listing their residence for sale.

9. What best describes a 'customer' in a real estate transaction?

a) This is the same as a client, or in other words, this is the person whom the real estate agent represents.

b) Someone that is not in a brokerage relationship with that agent, but the agent might perform ministerial acts for them in a transaction.

c) A customer is someone that you've shown houses to, but they have not yet purchased a property.

d) A customer is someone that is listing their property For Sale By Owner (FSBO).

10. What is designated agency?

a) This is where the broker will designate an agent in their firm to represent the seller and another agent in the same firm to represent the buyer.

b) This is where one agent will represent both the buyer and seller of the same transaction.

c) This is where an agent will work as a limited services agent for a client.

d) This where an agent will place the property on the MLS for a fixed fee.

11. Which best describes intra company agency?

a) When one real estate agent represents both parties in a deal

b) When a client agrees to a limited-service brokerage agreement

c) When one real estate brokerage represents both parties in a deal, but each side is represented by a different real estate agent within the brokerage

d) When a client is looking only to get their property listed on the MLS and does not need a full-service agent

12. What is true in regard to unintentional misrepresentation?

a) The agent has no liability in this matter since it was an honest mistake.

b) The agent is considered negligent because they either knew or should have known about the misrepresentation.

c) The agent must present their case to VREB.

d) The principal broker must release the agent from the brokerage if they are found guilty of unintentional misrepresentation.

13. What is a requirement of brokerage agreements in Virginia?

a) They must be in writing.

b) They can only be for a maximum of 6 months.

c) They only need to be done when listing a property for sale.

d) They can go on a month-to-month basis.

14. Which is an example of intentional misrepresentation?

a) If a listing agent knows the seller has had flooding or foundation issues in the past on their property and fails to disclose it when asked about it

b) If a listing agent claims that the house is the 'nicest house in the neighborhood.'

c) If a listing agent says the house will appreciate 10% over the next 5 years

d) If a listing agent discloses that the previous seller has HIV/AIDS

15. What must happen if an agent is listing their own property for sale?

a) This is not allowed; they would have to use a separate agent.

b) They are allowed to list their property but will not make a commission from it.

c) They must disclose that they are a licensed agent.

d) They can choose whether or not they want to put a for sale sign in their yard.

16. What is true in regard to aircraft noise disclosures for selling a property?

a) Virginia is a 'buyer beware' state, so no disclosure is needed.

b) If the property is subject to a noise zone, then a seller is required to disclose this information.

c) A seller only needs to disclose this information if they are asked directly by a buyer or agent.

d) Properties subject to noise zones tend to sell for 10%-20% below market value.

17. If a property was used to manufacture meth, what type of disclosure is required?

a) If a house was used to make meth and it was not properly remediated, then it must be disclosed. If it was used to manufacture meth but then property remediated, then no disclosure is needed.

b) No disclosure is necessary. It is up to the buyer and their home inspector to discover any defects.

c) If there was ever meth manufactured in the property, it must be disclosed.

d) Meth houses are functionally obsolete and must be torn down and rebuilt.

18. What is a seller's disclosure requirement if they own a stigmatized property?

a) Sellers in Virginia are not required to disclose anything since it is a 'buyer beware' state.

b) If there is no effect on the structure of the property, then sellers don't have to disclose any events such as hauntings, homicides, death, or felonies.

c) Sellers in Virginia are required to disclose anything that could have an adverse effect on selling a home, even if it's not a structural or material defect.

d) Sellers only have to disclose if the property is stigmatized if the potential buyer asks them.

19. What is it known as when a broker mixes personal funds with escrow funds?

a) Conversion

b) Amortization

c) Co-mingling

d) Prepaid interest

20. What is an acceptable form of deposit in regard to the earnest money?

a) So long as both parties agree to it in writing, it can be any form of payment.

b) Cash

c) Check

d) Wire transfer

21. How many days does a landlord have to return a security deposit?

a) 30 days

b) 45 days

c) 14 days

d) 60 days

22. What type of funds should be put in the broker's escrow account?

a) Commission checks from the transaction

b) Money for repairs from the home inspection list

c) Bonus commission from one agent to another for a job well done on the transaction

d) Earnest money deposits only

23. How much will licensees be assessed if the transaction recovery fund falls below the minimum amount?

a) $20
b) $50
c) $100
d) $10

24. What type of services can an unlicensed assistant legally perform?

a) 'Ministerial acts' which are routine acts that do not involve a licensee's judgment or expertise
b) Buying, selling, or leasing a property
c) Negotiating a real estate deal for a buyer
d) Preparing a real estate contract

25. What is the benefit of submitting an audit report to VREB every 3 years?

a) This is a requirement; brokers who do not submit every 3 years are subject to fines.
b) VREB will give full reimbursement for the amount of the brokerage VREB yearly dues for every 3-year period.
c) Principal brokers receive immunity from VREB enforcement actions.

d) VREB will give voting power to the Principal Brokers who submit an audit report every 3 years.

26. What is true in regard to the buyer selecting a settlement agent for a closing?

a) The buyer can choose any title company they want.

b) The seller always chooses the title company.

c) Both the seller and buyer have to agree on the settlement agent.

d) The settlement agent must be affiliated with at least one of the real estate brokerages in the transaction.

27. Can a broker or agent represent both a buyer and seller in the same transaction?

a) No, this is illegal in Virginia.

b) Yes, it happens all the time and no further agreements are necessary.

c) No, a buyer and seller in the same transaction must be represented by different real estate companies.

d) Yes, an agent or broker can represent both buyer and seller so long as they have written consent from both the buyer and seller.

28. What is the main purpose of the Virginia Real Estate Board (VREB)?

a) To enforce fair housing laws

b) To make sure HOAs and condo associations are in compliance

c) It oversees real estate licensure in Virginia.

d) To do a yearly audit of real estate brokerages

29. During a brokerage audit, all of the following are checked, except for what?

a) Proper handling of escrow deposits

b) Advertising and media in all forms

c) The use of unlicensed individuals

d) The ranking of the highest-earning agents in the office

30. What are the continuing education requirements for principal brokers?

a) 24 hours every 2 years

b) 16 hours every year

c) 24 hours every year

d) 16 hours every 2 years

31. What is true in regard to referral fees?

a) Referral fees can be given at any time in exchange for sending over a good deal.

b) Referral fees are not allowed in real estate under any circumstance.

c) An agent is not allowed to pay referral fees to a friend who does not have a license.

d) Anyone can earn a referral fee so long as the principal broker signs off on it.

32. Can a broker be licensed with two brokerages at the same time?

a) No, you are only allowed to be licensed under one brokerage.

b) Yes, so long as there is permission from both brokers and files for concurrent licensure with VREB.

c) Yes, you can be licensed with as many brokerages as you choose to be.

d) No, Virginia is a state that does not allow this.

33. Who is ultimately responsible for supervising real estate advertising at a brokerage?

a) The licensee creating the advertising

b) Associate brokers must oversee the advertising.

c) The owner of the brokerage

d) The principal broker

34. What is not allowed in real estate advertising, according to the Virginia Fair Housing Laws?

a) Advertising for a specific race
b) Advertising for a specific religion
c) Advertising for 'adults only'
d) All of the above

35. A standard brokerage relationship is between which parties?

a) The brokerage and the client
b) The salesperson and client
c) The associate broker and the client
d) The real estate team and the client

36. Who creates the residential disclosure statement?

a) HOA board
b) National Association of Realtors
c) Real estate board
d) DPOR

37. Who is responsible for providing a resale and disclosure packet for an HOA/POA?

a) Seller
b) Buyer
c) The HOA
d) The realtor

38. Which of the following is one of the duties of a real estate agent?

a) They have to find real estate deals at least 10% under market value.

b) They must deliver transactional documents in a deal promptly.

c) They have to recommend the best title companies and lender.

d) They must present all available properties to a client including auction homes that meet the buyer's criteria.

39. The majority of the time, real estate agents are considered what?

a) Independent contractors within the brokerage

b) Employees under the brokerage

c) Minority partners within the brokerage

d) Self-employed with no brokerage affiliation

40. When a seller is selling a property with no agent, what is still true?

a) Since there is no listing agreement, the seller does not need to disclose any info

b) The seller must still fill out a property disclosure form for the buyer.

c) They must still offer a commission to a buyer's agent.

d) They are not allowed to put the property on the MLS.

ANSWER KEY TO EXAM 4

1. A, Include an up-to-date list of all the timeshare owners in that community

2. B, 72 hours

3. D, $150 for a hard copy, $125 for an electronic copy

4. D, Taking a property through eminent domain to create a public park or area

5. C, Virginia Common Interest Community Board

6. A, You are allowed to refuse a rental to a felon so long as all the potential tenants were treated the same way

7. A, It is investigated by the Virginia Fair Housing Office; however, the VREB will discipline licensees for violations.

8. A, This is when one agent represents both the buyer and seller in the same transaction.

9. B, Someone that is not in a brokerage relationship with that agent, but the agent might perform ministerial acts for them in a transaction

10. A, This is where the broker will designate an agent in their firm to represent the seller and another agent in the same firm to represent the buyer.

11. C, When one real estate brokerage represents both parties in a deal, but each side is represented by a different real estate agent within the brokerage.

12. B, The agent is considered negligent because they either knew or should have known about the misrepresentation.

13. A, They must be in writing.

14. A, If a listing agent knows the seller has had flooding or foundation issues in the past on their property and fails to disclose it when asked about it

15. C, They must disclose that they are a licensed agent.

16. B, If the property is subject to a noise zone, then a seller is required to disclose this information

17. A, If a seller knows the house was used to make meth and it was not properly remediated, then these facts must be disclosed. If it was used to manufacture but then property remediated, then no disclosure is needed.

18. B, If there is no effect on the structure of the property, then sellers don't have to disclose any events such as hauntings, homicides, death, or felonies.

19. C, Co-mingling

20. A, So long as both parties agree to it in writing, it can be any form of payment, even a promissory note.

21. B, 45 days

22. D, Earnest money deposits only

23. A, $20

24. A, 'Ministerial acts,' which are routine acts that do not involve a licensee's judgment or expertise

25. C, Principal brokers receive immunity from VREB enforcement actions.

26. A, The buyer can choose any title company they want.

27. D, Yes, an agent or broker can represent both buyer and seller so long as they have written consent from both the buyer and seller.

28. C, It oversees real estate licensure in Virginia.

29. D, The ranking of the highest-earning agents in the office

30. A, 24 hours every 2 years

31. C, An agent is not allowed to pay referral fees to a friend who does not have a license

32. B, Yes, so long as there is permission from both brokers and files for concurrent licensure with VREB

33. D, The principal broker

34. D, All of the above

35. A, The brokerage and the client

36. C, Real estate board

37. A, Seller

38. B, Must deliver transactional documents in a deal promptly

39. A, Independent contractors within the brokerage

40. B, The seller must still fill out a property disclosure form for the buyer.

PRACTICE EXAM 5

1. **Where does the excess of the balance of the Transaction Recovery fund go if the fund exceeds 2 million?**

   a) The Virginia Housing Trust Fund
   b) The real estate commission
   c) The Virginia real estate board
   d) The National Association of Realtors

2. **What is the education requirement for becoming a real estate salesperson?**

   a) You must have graduated from a 2- or 4-year college and have 60 hours of training from a qualifying real estate course.
   b) You must have at least a high school diploma or equivalent and 60 hours of training from a qualifying real estate course.
   c) You must have a high school diploma or equivalent and 40 hours of training from a qualifying real estate course.
   d) You must have graduated from a 4-year university and have 50 hours of training from a qualifying real estate course.

3. How many hours of post-license education must new Virginia salespersons take in their first renewal period?

    a)   16 hours

    b)   24 hours

    c)   60 hours

    d)   30 hours

4. Which of the following statements best describes a net listing?

    a)   They are illegal, and it's when a broker would keep the difference between the listing price and the final sales price.

    b)   They are allowed in Virginia, and it's when a broker would keep the difference between the listing price and final sales price.

    c)   A net listing is when an agent puts the property on the MLS for a fixed fee regardless of whether the property sells.

    d)   A net listing is also known as a limited-service brokerage agreement.

5. Can a client or salesperson pay a bonus to a licensee at closing if they did an excellent job?

    a)   No, this is an illegal kickback.

    b)   Yes, they can give any amount they want.

c) Yes, but only if it goes through the broker, who can then give it to the salesperson.

d) No, only the amount listed on the real estate agreement can be given to an agent.

6. What is one requirement of all real estate advertising?

a) It must have the brokerage name or a link to the name.

b) It must have the company logo.

c) It must have the cell phone number of the listing agent.

d) It must have the amount of commission clearly advertised.

7. Failing to handle an earnest money deposit properly is known as what?

a) Omission

b) Improper delivery of instruments

c) Misrepresentation

d) Bait and switch

8. How long does an agent have to keep records of real estate transactions?

a) 5 years

b) 1 year

c) No time limit

d) 3 years

9. How many days do you have to notify the VREB of any changes in names or addresses?

a) 30 days

b) 14 days

c) 10 days

d) 60 days

10. All of the following are ways that money can be disbursed from a broker's escrow account, except what?

a) Settlement

b) Court order

c) The unilateral decision of the principal broker on the buyer's side

d) Agreement of all parties in writing

11. How many days does a broker have to report improper conduct of an escrow account by one of their licensees to the Virginia Real Estate Board?

a) 3 business days

b) 5 business days

c) 7 business days

d) 10 business days

12. Do escrow accounts need to bear interest?

a) Yes, and it gets split between the buyer and seller.

b) No, but if they do, the broker must disclose in writing to all the parties how the interest will be distributed before ratification.

c) Yes, and the buyer is entitled to all interest amounts.

d) No, the escrow deposit must be put in a non-interest-bearing account.

13. Which of the following best describes a stigmatized property?

a) A property that has been condemned by the jurisdiction because of structural or mold issues

b) A home that was built before 1960 and has had at least 4 previous owners

c) A property that is being taken by the government's power of eminent domain to turn into a public area

d) A home where something has occurred, such as a death, crime, or haunting, which has no physical effect on the property

14. If a seller provides the property disclosure after going under contract, how many days does the buyer have to cancel the sale?

  a) Any time before closing since the seller failed to deliver the required disclosures before going under contract
  b) Within 3 days after the disclosures were delivered if it was done in person or by email, and within 5 days if they were delivered by regular mail
  c) Within 7 days after going under contract
  d) Within 10 days after going under contract

15. Before advertising a seller's property, what needs to happen?

  a) Agents and brokerages need to get the written consent of the seller or landlord.
  b) The agent needs to hire a marketing firm to promote the property.
  c) The seller needs to complete all the updates that the licensee recommends.
  d) The property needs to be put in the MLS.

16. What is the time frame for a buyer's recourse against a seller due to undisclosed or misrepresented defects after buying a house?

a) They can take recourse at any time; however, sooner is always better.
b) Within 3 years of settlement or occupancy
c) Within 1 year of settlement or occupancy
d) There is no recourse once you have closed on the property.

17. Who must supervise real estate advertising according to the VREB?

a) The managing broker must supervise all advertising.
b) Each licensed agent is responsible for making sure they don't violate any advertising rules.
c) Associate brokers have a duty to ensure property advertising.
d) There are no supervision requirements in regard to advertising.

18. If there are no real estate agents in a deal, what must be done with the property disclosure form?

a) The seller does not need to fill it out
b) The seller does not need to fill it out but should still give the potential buyer a verbal heads-up about the condition of the property.
c) It is recommended that the seller fill it out, but it is not necessary.

d) The seller must still fill out the form and give it to the buyer.

19. Which of the following does a seller have to disclose to a buyer?

a) An old piping system in a house
b) Any pending building or zoning violations
c) A functioning septic system that does not require a waiver
d) A furnace that is past its life expectancy but still functioning

20. For sale signs in Virginia must include what information?

a) The name of the brokerage
b) The firm name and office phone number
c) A phone number or website address of the brokerage
d) There are no advertising requirements on signs for real estate agents.

21. What is the Virginia Law which regulates disclosure requirements for a sale of a property?

a) Virginia Property Disclosure Act
b) The Virginia Fair Housing Act
c) The Virginia Transaction Recovery Fund
d) The Virginia Real Estate Cooperative Act

22. All of the following are acceptable ways a brokerage relationship can be terminated except for what?

    a) Completion of the transaction in accordance with the contract
    b) A mutually agreed upon termination of the brokerage agreement
    c) A date of expiration as agreed upon in the brokerage agreement
    d) A unilateral decision by either the client or agent to stop working together

23. If an unrepresented party is buying or selling a property from an agent, then what is required?

    a) Nothing is required, since they have no agent.
    b) The agent who is working the deal must have them fill out a limited-service agent agreement.
    c) The agent must have the other party fill out an unrepresented party form.
    d) The unrepresented party must fill out a dual agency disclosure.

24. What is one of the requirements of all brokerage agreements?

    a) It must specify the terms and conditions of the services being offered.

b) It must be at least a 6 month agreement.

c) Brokerage agreements are only necessary for listing a property.

d) All brokerage requirements will vary depending on the brokerage

25. What happens if the brokerage agreement does not have a definite termination date?

a) It is not a valid agreement, and it is null and void.

b) The agreement will terminate 90 days after the date of the agreement.

c) The agreement will continue until the property is sold or the client requests to void the agreement.

d) The agreement will continue on a month-to-month basis until closing or until either party sends notice to void the agreement.

26. What is the standard length of time for a brokerage agreement?

a) Whatever time period the client and the broker agree to. Virginia law does not have a specified time.

b) 30 days

c) 6 months

d) 1 year

27. **What is a requirement of dual agency as well as designated agency?**

    a) Verbal acknowledgment of all parties involved

    b) Written consent of the principal broker

    c) Written consent of all the parties involved

    d) Written consent of at least the buyer or seller in the transaction

28. **How many days after the death or disability of a licensed real estate broker who was the owner of the brokerage do you have to close out the business?**

    a) 180 days

    b) 90 days

    c) 365 days

    d) As long as necessary

29. **What does the Virginia condo act do?**

    a) It sets the yearly condo fees for associations across Virginia.

    b) It investigates fair housing violations in condos and cooperatives.

    c) It provides condominium resale documents and disclosures.

    d) It establishes the laws for condo owners and owner associations.

30. How many days does a buyer of a Timeshare have to cancel?

a) 7 days
b) 3 days
c) 5 days
d) 10 days

31. What must a seller disclose if they are in a military accident-prone area?

a) A seller only has to disclose information if there has been an incident in regard to military accidents while they have owned the property.
b) No disclosure is necessary since this is a buyer beware state.
c) For sale by owner sellers do not need to disclose this information; however, sellers represented by an agent must disclose this.
d) Sellers need to disclose that they are in a military accident-prone area.

32. What must be on a licensee's business card?

a) Name and phone number
b) Name and the website and phone number of the brokerage
c) Name, firm name, and contact information
d) There are no requirements for a licensee's business card

33. Which groups are protected under the Fair Housing Law?

    a) Race, color, religion, national origin, sex, elderliness, familial status, and disability

    b) Race, color, religion, national origin, sex, marital status, alcoholism, and disability

    c) Race, color, religion, students, elderliness, familial status, and sexual orientation

    d) Race, color, religion, drug addicts, elderliness, sexual orientation, and disability

34. A homeowner who lives in a POA (Property Owner's Association) has all of the following rights, except what?

    a) Accessing the financial records of the POA

    b) Voting on POA issues

    c) Serving on the POA board assuming they get elected and are in good standing

    d) Receiving referral money from a licensed agent for finding out who is selling their property next

35. With unrepresented parties, what is an agent allowed to do?

    a) Only ministerial duties that don't require expert guidance or advice

b) Negotiate on their behalf

c) Suggest terms of the contract that could make their offer more appealing

d) Since the other party is unrepresented the agent is allowed to do anything on behalf of their client so long as it's not illegal or misrepresentation.

36. VREB has the authority to do all of the following, except what?

a) Suspend, revoke, or deny a license renewal

b) Impose a fine on a licensee

c) Impose a jail sentence for fraud or another intentional misdoing

d) Send cease and desist orders to agents and brokers

37. What would be an example of improper dealing?

a) Putting a for sale sign on a property without the owner's consent

b) Putting a property on the MLS for a flat fee

c) Working as a limited-service agent for a client

d) Having a license at multiple real estate brokerages

38. Which country was notorious for manufacturing defective drywall between the time periods of 2004-2007?

a) China
b) Mexico
c) United States
d) Germany

39. How many days does an HOA/POA have to deliver the resale and disclosure packets upon the request of a seller?

a) 3 days
b) 7 days
c) 14 days
d) 10 days

40. What is the Planning District 15 disclosure?

a) If your property had any mining activity or abandoned mines
b) If your property is in an environmental protection area
c) If your property is in a military air installation area
d) If your property was previously used to manufacture methamphetamines

1. A, The Virginia Housing Trust Fund

2. B, You must have at least a high school diploma or equivalent and 60 hours of training from a qualifying real estate course

3. D, 30 hours

4. A, They are illegal, and it's when a broker would keep the difference between the listing price and the final sales price.

5. C, Yes, but only if it goes through the broker who can then give it to the salesperson.

6. A, It must have the brokerage name or a link to the name.

7. B, Improper delivery of instruments

8. D, 3 years

9. A, 30 days

10. C, The unilateral decision of the principal broker on the buyer's side

11. A, 3 business days

12. B, No, but if they do, the broker must disclose in writing to all the parties how the interest will be distributed before ratification.

13. D, A home where something has occurred, such as a death, crime, or haunting, which has no physical effect on the property.

14. B, Within 3 days after the disclosures were delivered if it was done in person or by email, and within 5 days if they were delivered by regular mail

15. A, Agents and brokerages need to get the written consent of the seller or landlord.

16. C, Within 1 year of settlement or occupancy

17. A, The managing broker must supervise all advertising

18. D, The seller must still fill out the form and give it to the buyer.

19. B, Pending building or zoning violations

20. B, They need to have the firm name and office phone number.

21. A, Virginia Property Disclosure Act

22. D, A unilateral decision by either the client or agent to stop working together

23. C, The agent must have the other party fill out an unrepresented party form

24. A, It must specify the terms and conditions of the services being offered.

25. B, The agreement will terminate 90 days after the date of the agreement.

26. A, Whatever time period agreed to by the client and the broker. Virginia law does not have a specified time.

27. C, Written consent of all the parties involved

28. A, 180 days

29. D, It establishes the laws for condo owners and owner associations.

30. A, 7 days

31. D, Yes, they are required to disclose.

32. C, Name, firm name, and contact information

33. A, Race, color, religion, national origin, sex, elderliness, familial status, and disability

34. D, Receiving referral money from a licensed agent for finding out who is selling their property next

35. A, Only ministerial duties that don't require expert guidance or advice

36. C, Impose a jail sentence for fraud or another intentional misdoing

37. A, Putting a for sale sign on a property without the owner's consent

38. A, China

39. C, 14 days

40. A, If your property had any mining activity or abandoned mines

NEXT STEPS

You have reached the end of this guide. For further training materials, please visit www.therealestate trainingteam.com to stay up to date with our real estate training education programs. If you enjoyed this guide, please also leave a helpful review on Amazon. Below, we provided a glossary that will help increase your knowledge and understanding for both the state and national portions of the exam.

GLOSSARY

1031 exchange. Also known as a like-kind exchange, it is the swapping of one piece of real property for another. This is a popular tactic for real estate investors to allow their investments to grow without being subject to capital gains tax.

203K loan. As a sub-type of the FHA loan, a 203K loan allows individuals to finance two significant purposes with a solitary loan – buying a home, and handling the needed repairs.

Absorption. Also known as the absorption rate, this is a calculation that determines how long it will take to sell the homes currently on the market. In real estate, the absorption rate is used to forecast market activity and prices.

Abstract of title. An abstract of title is a summary that includes any legal activity, documents, and rulings of a specific property. Whenever a title search is performed on a property, there will usually be an abstract of the title to go along with it.

Abstractor. Also known as an abstractor of title, this person analyzes and keeps records of abstracts of titles.

Any time a new deed transfer or any other legal activity occurs on a property, an abstractor handles the records.

Acceleration clause. An acceleration clause is a contract stipulation which states that a loan can be due in full if specific criteria are not met. Common examples that would put an acceleration clause in effect include a missed payment, failure to pay property taxes, and a lack of homeowner's insurance.

Accredited investor. An entity or person who has been deemed capable of handling the increased risks associated with specific investment offerings. An accredited investor holds the best choices when it comes to investment alternatives beyond exchange-listed securities.

ADA. ADA stands for the Americans with Disabilities Act of 1990, a civil rights law that protects citizens with disabilities from discrimination. In real estate, an agent or owner of a property may not discriminate against those with disabilities in regard to buying, leasing, or renting real property.

Addendum. An addendum is a stipulation, omission, or addition to a legal contract or document. Regarding real estate, an addendum can include financing or a contingency agreement.

Adverse possession. Adverse possession is when someone utilizes someone else's land without permission, but acquires ownership of land after a period of time. For example, if a landowner accidentally overextends his fence into his neighbor's property, he may acquire the land via adverse possession, even if it was an accident.

Affidavit. A written declaration or statement, sworn to before someone who holds the authority to bestow an oath.

Amenities. A property's features that make it more attractive and valuable to prospective tenants or buyers.

Amortization schedule. A detailed table of how a mortgage's monthly payments are applied to the loan, i.e., interest vs. principal. In a typical amortization schedule, the initial payments are mostly applied towards the interest.

Amortization. The loan payment comprises of a part that will be applied to pay the resulting interest on a loan, with the balance being applied to the principal. The interest portion lowers over time as the loan balance reduces, and the amount applied to the principal increases, thus helping the loan being paid off within the specified time.

Antitrust laws. Antitrust laws are competitive market laws that were put in place to protect consumers from unethical or illegal business practices involving a lack of competition. In regard to real estate, an example of an antitrust violation would be two major brokers deciding to represent clients in two separate territories in a city.

Appraisal process. An appraisal process is the professional estimate of the value of a property. Example: Lenders require an appraisal before they will grant a mortgage.

Appraised value. An appraised value is provided by an appraiser, which determines an estimated value of real property at a specific moment in time. In real estate, an appraisal can vary depending on the market value of homes in the area, as well as the demand for homes in your neighborhood.

Appurtenances. Appurtenances are anything that is attached to a piece of property that is passed on when the property is sold. Examples of appurtenances are furnaces or underground pools.

APR. APR stands for Annual Percentage Rate, which is the rate of interest charged on a loan on an annual basis.

For example, when a credit card offers an introductory APR of 1%, that is the Annual Percentage Rate.

Area of competence. An area of competence is the market, industry, or subject where one shows a certain level of expertise. In real estate, an agent with a history of residential sales can claim that real estate is an area of competence.

ARM loan. ARM means Adjustable Rate Mortgage, which refers to a loan with variable interest rates that can fluctuate depending on the market rate. Fluctuating interest rates can mean higher payments for a borrower, and are in contrast to a fixed mortgage rate.

Arm's length transaction. An arm's length transaction is when the buyer and the seller both act in their own self-interest without any interference or pressure from another party. In real estate, the buyer tries to pay the least for a home, and the seller is trying to maximize their sale price.

As is. In real estate, an "as is" listing is real property in which the seller refuses to make any repairs or offer any credits. Typically, as-is homes are offered at a significant discount compared to other homes in good condition.

Asbestos. Asbestos consists of six natural silicate materials that were commonly used as building insulation until it was discovered to be a severe health hazard. It was banned from use in real estate in the 1970s. Inhalation of asbestos can cause lung disease and cancer, as well as other respiratory issues.

Assemblage. Assemblage is when two or more adjoining lots are made into one large tract. Example: A developer could use assemblage to create a tract home community.

Assessed value. In real estate, an assessed value is utilized by the local/state government to determine property taxes. Factors such as comparable home values in the area, and recent appraisals play a role in determining a property's assessed value.

Associate broker. A licensed broker whose license is held by a principal broker, similar to a salespersons license. He or she is considered to be a real estate broker but is still supervised by and works for another broker.

Assumption clause. An assumption clause is a contract stipulation that allows a home seller to transfer their mortgage to the buyer. For example, in an assumption clause, the buyer essentially takes over the mortgage of a home.

Automated underwriting system. A technology-driven underwriting method that offers a computer-generated loan decision. This process is utilized in different capacities across the lending landscape.

Backup contract. A backup offer refers to additional offers after an original offer is accepted. A backup contract protects the seller in case the first offer falls through. For a buyer, a backup contract brings the opportunity to buy a home they might have given up on purchasing otherwise.

Balloon mortgage. A mortgage that holds a final payment larger than other payments. For instance, a 30-year loan due in 5 years would have a payment that pays it off over 30 years. However, as the loan would be due in 5 years, it would make the final payment larger than previous payments.

Bilateral agreement. In a bilateral agreement, there are two parties involved in a transaction. In regard to real estate, a bilateral agreement is usually between the buyer and the seller.

Biweekly payment mortgage. A kind of mortgage loan where payments are made every two weeks instead of every month. The payment is exactly one half of the monthly payment amount.

Blanket mortgage. Also known as a blanket loan, a blanket mortgage is a loan meant for more than one real estate property. For example, blanket mortgages are popular with real estate developers in a subdivision.

Blighted property. The legal term for a land that is in an unsafe, unsightly, and dilapidated condition. Different criteria are used by different states to determine whether a property should be classified as blighted.

Blockbusting. Blockbusting is the unethical practice of agents convincing white homeowners to sell their homes at below-market prices with the fear of minorities moving into the community. As a result, these agents sell these homes to minorities at higher prices. Although blockbusting was common before the Civil Rights Act, it is a rare occurrence today.

BPO. A broker price opinion (BPO) is similar to a real estate appraisal; the broker is typically hired by a bank or company to give their opinion for the value of a property. Example: The BPO helps determine the potential selling price for a property.

Breach of contract. A breach of contract is a failure to complete one or several terms within the contract. For example, if a seller decides to accept a better offer on their home after a deal has been made (with no backup offers allowed), the seller would be in breach of contract.

Bridge loans. Bridge loans are short-term loans that provide immediate cash flow, which provides a 'bridge' between one home and another. For example, if you are selling your home and buying another, a bridge loan would provide the adequate cash you need to secure the down payment on the next house while it is being sold.

Buffer zones. Neutral, vacant areas where any real estate development is prohibited. This is a technique used to create a neutral space between two different types of properties to minimize disturbances. Examples of buffer zones include small grassy areas in between commercial buildings and nature conservation areas.

Builder warranty. A type of insurance that is theoretically supposed to provide cover to protect the owner/buyer under circumstances where they are having trouble with work that has been done (or not done) by the builder.

Building codes. Sets of rules and regulations which govern the design, construction, and maintenance of buildings. Additionally, these regulations are the minimum requirements to ensure the safety and well-being of the building's occupants.

Bundle of rights. In real estate, the bundle of rights refers to the legal privileges afforded to a buyer in a transaction. Examples of a bundle of rights include the right of possession, the right of exclusion, and the right of disposition.

Buy-down. A payment made to the lender by the third party, buyer, seller, or some combination of these, making the lender get a lower interest rate during the early years of a loan. Usually, the buy-down is applicable for the first 1 to 5 years of a loan.

Buyer's right of redemption in a foreclosure. A buyer's right of redemption allows a borrower to buy their home back after foreclosure from the individual who purchased the home at auction. In other cases, a right of redemption may also include the homeowner being able to pay back the mortgage within a specified amount of time.

CAN-SPAM Act. CAN-SPAM stands for Controlling the Assault of Non-Solicited Pornography and Marketing Act of 2003. In regard to real estate, brokers and agents must follow the guidelines of CAN-SPAM, which include: marketing e-mails must consist of accurate information, the subject lines must reflect the contents, a mailing address must be included, and your subscribers must be able to opt out of e-mails easily.

Cap rate calculation. Calculating the cap rate is done by dividing the Net Operating Income by the market value of a property. For example, if the NOI is $10,000, and the value of the property is $50,000, the cap rate is 5 percent.

Cap rate. A cap rate (or capitalization rate) is used in commercial real estate to determine the expected rate of return on an investment. Example: When a lender is considering a deal, the cap rate has a significant influence on their decision.

Carbon monoxide. An odorless, colorless, and tasteless flammable gas that can be harmful to humans and other animals at a high enough concentration. In real estate, common occurrences of carbon monoxide poisoning include faulty water heaters and furnaces.

Cash on cash return. This refers to a rate of return used often in real estate transactions, which calculates the cash income received on the cash invested in a real estate property. This metric is typically used to evaluate commercial real estate investment performance.

Caveat emptor. Often translated into buyer beware, caveat emptor is a legal principle that states a buyer is the sole party responsible for checking and observing the quality of a product or service before a purchase is made. In real estate, when a buyer is finding a house, the responsibility is on the buyer to inspect the quality of the home and see any potential repairs/damage.

Chain of title. The chain of title illustrates the different instances where the deed or title of a property has been transferred. Since homes can date back 100+ years, the chain of title is essential to ensure there are no discrepancies in the past ownership of property.

Characteristics of land. Three characteristics of land are immobility, indestructibility, and uniqueness.

Clear title. A clear title is a real property title that does not have any liens from lenders or claims to ownership in court. When buyers are searching for real estate to purchase, a clear title is the most desirable.

Client. A client has a contractual relationship with a real estate agent. The agent is the representative of the client in the purchase or sale of a property. An example of a client is a person who has signed a buyer's agreement with a real estate agent. The agent will handle the real estate transaction on the client's behalf and is legally entitled to a percent of the sale price.

Closing disclosure. A closing disclosure provides the final details concerning a mortgage loan. Example: A closing disclosure includes loan terms, monthly payments, and closing costs.

Cloud on title. Any defect or irregularity in a title that may deem a property unfit for sale. Examples include a lien or pending lawsuit and are usually found during a title search.

CMA. A Comparative Market Analysis (CMA) is the method that is used for homeowners to learn their property's current home value; it is an in-depth analysis of a home's worth. Example: A CMA is used when a real estate agent is listing a home.

Collateral. Collateral is the promise of property or other assets in an effort to secure financing. For example, land can be used as collateral when a borrower tries to secure a mortgage.

Collusion. Collusion is defined as the act of cooperating in a conspiracy-like matter. In real estate, agents who attempt to manipulate offers from a lender to create a favorable commission would be in collusion with the mortgage lender.

Commingling. Commingling is the illegal act of mixing a client's funds, such as an earnest money deposit with the agent's personal funds.

Commission split. Commission splits occur when there are multiple parties involved in a sale. In regard to real estate, when an agent sells a home for the client, the agent splits the commission with the broker, either 50/50, 70/30, or somewhere in between.

Comparable sales. Also referred to as comps, comparable sales are used to determine a home or commercial property's value by comparing homes with similar characteristics and in an area. As an example, when a seller wants to figure out how much to list their home for, comps provide a general idea of the value of homes similar to theirs in the neighborhood.

Concession. A discount or benefit offered by the seller or buyer to assist in selling a house and closing a deal. These are generally specified during negotiations and are included in closing costs.

Condemnation. In real estate, condemnation is the seizure of private property for public use in exchange for compensation. While eminent domain illustrates the state's right to seize property, condemnation refers to the actions of taking property.

Condo conversion. The process of dividing real estate property held under one title into individually owned units that share common elements like a lobby, exterior walls, recreational facilities, etc.

Condo docs. A variety of documents that establish a condominium and regulate living in a condominium community. These describe things like the location of the condo, responsibilities of the unit owners, etc.

Condominium. More commonly referred to as a condo, condominiums are residences that typically share walls with other units, but are sold individually. The individual sale of a condominium is what makes them different from apartments, which can be rented only.

Confidentiality. Confidentiality is the act or state of keeping information private. In real estate, confidentiality agreements are usually signed to protect the identity of a seller in a real estate transaction.

Conflict of interest. A conflict of interest occurs when an agent's personal or professional interest works in contrast to a client's. One of the most common examples where Conflicts of Interests occur are Owner/Agent real estate listings.

Conforming loan. A conforming loan is a housing loan that does not exceed the conforming loan limit set by Freddie Mac and Fannie Mae. In 2019, a mortgage loan of less than $484,350 was considered to be a conforming loan.

Construction loans. Construction loans are loans that are used for building property or properties. These loans are shorter-term than a typical mortgage and are also known as self-build loans.

Contingencies. In real estate, contingencies are criteria that need to be met for the transaction to be completed. For example, an offer can be accepted on a home with the contingency that they must sell their own house first.

Conversion. In real estate, conversion is the misappropriation of ownership rights on a property that belongs to someone else. For example, when an agent uses earnest money for their personal use, they are breaking the law via conversion.

Cooperative ownership. In cooperative ownership, owners don't own real estate but are considered shareholders in a corporation. The most common example is a co-op grocery store. The corporation 'owns' the store, and store ownership is comprised of shareholders.

Co-ownership. Co-ownership is when several people own interest in a real estate property. For example, if several family members own a rental property, this is an instance of co-ownership.

Cost approach. The cost approach is a valuation method that speculates the price a buyer should pay for a property should be equal to the cost to build another equivalent property. For example, when agents run comps for a client, they are using the cost approach.

Cost to cure method. The cost to cure method is the amount of money required to restore something that is depressing the value of the property. Example: If the shingles on the house are falling off and the cost to cure is $4,000, and the current condition has depreciated the house by $6,000, then the problem is curable.

Counteroffer. A counteroffer is simply an offer made in response to an offer from another party. For example, you receive an offer on your car for $10,000, but you reply with an offer to sell for $11,000; the latter is a counteroffer.

Covenant against encumbrances. A covenant against encumbrances is any issue that would hinder a property owner's ability to transfer title. Examples of encumbrances include liens, mortgages, and easements.

Covenant of quiet enjoyment. Similar to a covenant of warranty, quiet enjoyment ensures that a seller is responsible for any third-party legal claims. For example, if a third party attempts to foreclose on a property, the seller would be liable for any damages.

Covenant of warranty. A covenant states that a grantor will defend against any claims made against the title by a third party. Similar to a Quiet Enjoyment, a covenant of warranty assures that any legal claim would be the responsibility of the seller.

Covenants in a deed. Covenants and restrictions are regulations stipulated in a real estate title that provide certain rules and regulations on a specific property. An example of covenants and restrictions in a deed includes whether a home can have extra rooms added, or whether a patio or pool can be added to a backyard.

Crawl space. It is essentially a hollow area that is found under some homes between the first floor and the ground floor. Usually, it is roughly anywhere between 1 and 3 feet high – which is high enough for somebody to enter by crawling, as the name implies.

Credit history. Credit history is the record of an individual's past financial history in regard to financing. Typical credit history reports include payment history, any accounts in collections, closed accounts, and the amount of credit used.

Credit union. Financial cooperative developed by and for its members who are its borrowers, shareholders, and depositors. Being non-profit in nature, credit unions provide many banking services like commercial and consumer loans, guaranties, and credit cards, among others.

Curb appeal. A term used to describe the general attractiveness of a piece of real estate property from the sidewalk to prospective buyers. Realtors often use this term to evaluate or sell a piece of property.

Custom builder. Someone who develops a building for a specific owner, designing the property to cater to the owner's requirements, instead of building first and looking for a buyer afterwards.

Customer. A customer is someone who is making buying decisions; a buying decision is the process of evaluating the pros and cons of making a purchase. An example of a customer is a person that is looking to buy a home and asking a real estate agent questions while researching various properties.

Debt to income ratio. A personal finance measure which compares the debt payment of an individual to his/her overall income. It is a way lenders use to measure the ability of an individual to repay debts and manage monthly payments.

Deed in lieu of foreclosure. A deed in lieu of foreclosure provides an opportunity for a borrower to sign over ownership of a home to the lender and avoid foreclosure. Homeowners in danger of being foreclosed can utilize a deed in lieu of foreclosure instead of enduring the foreclosure process.

Deed of trust. A legal document utilized in various states in lieu of a mortgage. Here, a trustor transfers the property to a trustee, in favor of the lender, and re-conveyed after full payment is made.

Deed restrictions. Similar to covenants, restrictions in a deed can also include various uses of the home that may not be allowed. Restrictions can consist of using a home as a home or branch office.

Deed. A deed is a written, signed legal document that signifies ownership of real property. Whenever someone buys a home, the deed is transferred to reflect this change in ownership.

Deferred maintenance. Deferred maintenance is when repairs are postponed on a property to save costs. Example: A property needs a yearly heat and air checkup. If a property owner deferred this, at some point, they might have to spend much more money to replace the entire system.

Deficiency judgment against a borrower. This is a court ruling after a foreclosure, which states a foreclosure sale did not produce enough funds to repay the loan. In these instances, a deficiency judgment usually results in a lien placed against the borrower for the amount of money owed.

Deliberate misrepresentation. Deliberate misrepresentation is an intentional statement that is found to be untrue. In real estate, if an agent states that the roof of a home needed repairs, and it is shown that the agent had prior knowledge, this is an example of deliberate misrepresentation.

Depreciation. Depreciation is an asset's value decreasing over time. Common examples of goods that depreciate include cars and most sporting goods.

Designated agent. In a designated agent scenario, a buyer and seller each have their agent; however, those agents work for the same real estate company. This is different from dual agency since each principal in the transaction has their agent representing them. Although similar to dual agency, having a designated agent is a preferred form of transaction.

Difference between a real estate agent and a Realtor?. Real estate agents and Realtors are both licensed to sell real estate; however, not every real estate agent is a Realtor. Realtors must adhere to the Realtor code of ethics and be a member of the National Association of Realtors.

Difference between an appraisal and CMA. The difference between an appraisal and a CMA is that a real estate broker does a CMA, and a real estate appraiser does an appraisal. Example: A CMA is an estimate of a home's value for a listing; an appraisal is typically done when financing is necessary.

Disclosure of agency. A disclosure of agency provides details on the relationship between an agent and their client(s). It is a written description signed by the buyer or seller explaining the role that the agent will play in the transaction. This gives the buyer or seller transparency as to which party the agent is representing.

Disclosures of Material Facts. In real estate, material facts are known as facts that, if known, can alter the decision of a buyer's choice in a transaction. Examples of material facts include a recently-discovered mold issue or a damaged foundation. Each state will vary as to their disclosure laws; however, a good rule of thumb is to disclose any material information to avoid potential lawsuits later.

Discount points calculation. To calculate discount points, we will assume that paying 1 percent of the loan amount will reduce the APR by a quarter of a percent. Therefore, for a $100,000 loan, each point will cost $1000, and if the initial interest rate is 5 percent, one point would reduce the rate to 4.75 percent.

Distress sale. A sale of property in a situation when the seller is under huge pressure to sell. Usually, the property is sold at a price lower than its present market value.

Distressed property. A distressed property is any real property that is facing or under foreclosure. Anytime one sees a foreclosure option, one can assume it is a distressed property.

DOM. Also known as 'days on market.' It indicates the number of days a particular property has been for sale on the real estate market.

Dual agency. Dual agency is when a real estate agent acts as the listing agent and buyer's agent in a real estate transaction. This practice is illegal in several states, and because of the nature of the transaction, you must have an agreement in writing from both the buyer and seller that you will be a dual agent.

Due care. Due care is a legal term that refers to the amount of care and diligence a party takes to avoid causing harm to another. For example, a seller's agent will take the due care (or due diligence) to ensure that the home is in good financial standing, and an inspection is done to find any potential pitfalls.

Due diligence. Due diligence is the practice of research or investigation of an investment or business before signing a contract. For example, a title search is a form of due diligence.

Due on sale clause. A due on sale clause is a contract clause that provides the right to the lender to require that the remaining balance of a loan needs to be paid in full before a home sale or transfer of ownership occurs. The due on sale clause is in most mortgage contracts and is utilized as a means to avoid a homeowner being able to sell their house before paying the existing loan.

E and O insurance. This is Errors and Omission Insurance, which is professional liability insurance. In regard to real estate, E and O insurance provides liability coverage in the event a broker or agent demonstrates negligence or gives bad advice to a client.

Earnest money deposit. Earnest money is an act of good faith and is a sum deposited into an account to demonstrate a willingness to buy a home. For example, when a buyer needs the time necessary to secure financing, perform a home inspection and a home appraisal, an earnest money deposit is made.

Easements. Easements are a legal right to use someone else's land for a specific purpose. An example of an easement would be granting the electric company to use your property to run power lines.

Economic life. Economic life or useful life is the estimated lifespan of a fixed asset's depreciation. Example: The shingles on a roof have a useful life of ten years, depending on the climate.

Economic obsolescence. Economic obsolescence happens when a property value decreases due to external factors. Example: When a freeway is built right next to a neighborhood.

Eminent domain. Under eminent domain, the government has the right to purchase private property and convert it into public property. An example of eminent domain is when a property is purchased by the government to make room for an expanded highway.

Empty nesters. A term, in general, used to indicate parents whose children have left the house after growing up.

Encroachments. In real estate, encroachments occur when a property owner builds onto a neighbor's property. For example, if a homeowner was building a pool, and the hole dug for the pool crossed into his neighbor's property, this would be a form of encroachment.

Encumbrances. In real estate, an encumbrance can be any claim or impediment placed on real estate property. Examples of encumbrances include liens, mortgages, or private restrictions.

Equal Credit Opportunity Act. This is a law that was enacted in 1974 and prohibits a lender or creditor from discriminating against a borrower based on race, color, gender, national origin, age, or marital status. For example, if a creditor refuses a creditworthy applicant for a loan simply because they are not married, they violate the ECOA.

Equitable title. In real estate law, an equitable title usually refers to the financial stake one owns in a property, which differs from owning legal title. For example, an equitable titleholder cannot transfer ownership of the property without legal title.

Equity. Financial interest of a homeowner in a property. It's the difference between the amount still owed on the property's mortgage and other liens, and its fair market value.

Escalation clause. In real estate, an escalation clause means a prospective buyer has placed an offer, as well as a higher offer, should another bidder make an offer higher than the original one. For example, a buyer makes an offer of $50,000, with an escalation clause that, should someone make a better offer, the buyer is willing to increase their offer to as much as $80,000.

Escheat. This is a common-law practice in which property is transferred to the state when no heirs to the property are available. For example, if a property owner dies and does not have a will or any legal heirs, Escheat would grant ownership of the property to the state. This is often the last resort after all means of finding a viable successor to take ownership of the property have been exhausted.

Escrow account. In regard to real estate, a trust account (or escrow account) is an account managed by a third party during a transaction. For example, a buyer can place all the funds required before closing into an escrow account, which is handled by a separate party, usually an attorney.

Escrow agent. An escrow agent holds the earnest money deposit while a transaction is completed. In real estate, an attorney is usually an escrow agent.

Estate tax value. In federal tax law, estate taxes are levied on property and assets at their fair market value when an individual passes away. For example, if the deceased has assets valued over $11.4 million, estate taxes would apply even if the deceased paid less at the time of purchase.

Estates at sufferance. Estates at sufferance is a leasehold estate agreement in which a tenant occupies a property after the lease has expired, but before a landlord requests that they vacate. During this period, any rents due from the original lease agreement must be paid in an estates at sufferance situation.

Estates at will. Also known as a tenancy at will, this is a leasehold agreement where either party can terminate the lease as long as enough advance notice is given. In this instance, a tenancy at will may not require a contract, since either party can opt out at any time.

Estates for years. This is a form of leasehold estate where a tenant leases property for a specified period of time. One unique aspect of estates for years is that no notice is needed to vacate since the lease agreement states when the tenant must leave.

Exclusive agency. The method of offering one real estate broker the exclusive selling right to sell a specific property, though it may be agreed upon to pay a part of the sales commission to the broker who gets a buyer.

Exclusive right to sell listing. A real estate agent has exclusive rights to sell a home and is paid a commission even if the principal/client finds a buyer on their own. If a client enters into an exclusive right to sell with an agent, the client may not sign an agreement with any other agent to sell their home.

Executor. A person whose name is mentioned in a will to manage a deceased person's estate. The court appoints an administrator if no executor is named in a will. The feminine form is 'executrix.'

Fair housing act of 1968. Also known as Title VIII of the Civil Rights Act of 1968, this act protects families and individuals from discrimination in rental, sale, advertising of housing, or financing. It prohibits discrimination based on color, disability, race, religion, national origin, and family status.

Fair housing issues in advertising. Fair housing issues in advertising include any marketing or advertisements which show preference to a specific class based on race, gender, familial status, disability, religion, or national origin. For example, a home advertisement that restricts children is considered a violation of fair housing.

Fair market value. The highest price which a buyer, willing but not forced to buy, would pay, and the lowest which a seller, willing but not forced to sell, would accept.

Familial status. Familial status is when an adult/parent houses a child or guardian under the age of 18. Under FHA guidelines, landlords may not discriminate against renting homes to someone if they have minors in the household.

Fannie Mae. Fannie Mae is a common term that refers to the Federal National Mortgage Association, an entity sponsored by the U.S. Government. Fannie Mae's purpose is to provide secure mortgage loans to help more American citizens afford homes.

Fee simple. Fee simple is a type of freehold estate in which the owner of a property can use it to its fullest extent. A fee simple estate is the highest possible real estate ownership form.

FFHA. FFHA stands for the Federal Fair Housing Act, which is another way of saying the Fair Housing Act. The Federal Fair Housing Act was enacted as a part of the Civil Rights Act of 1968.

FHA loan. An FHA (Federal Housing Administration) loan is a mortgage issued by an FHA-approved lender and insured by the FHA for low-to-moderate-income borrowers. They require a lower down payment and lower credit score than most conventional loans. An example of an FHA loan being used would be a first-time homeowner with a low FICO score (even as low as 500) that has verifiable employment history for the last two years.

FHA. FHA is the Federal Housing Administration. They provide mortgage insurance on loans made by FHA-approved lenders. The FHA helps lenders with easy financing and low down payments.

FHFA. FHFA is the Federal Housing Finance Agency. The FHFA regulates Fannie Mae, Freddie Mac, and the Federal Home Loan Banks. Established in 2008, FHFA has filed a total of 18 lawsuits against financial institutions as of 2019.

Fiduciary duties to a principal/client. Fiduciary duties are legally mandated obligations that a real estate agent must abide by during a transaction. Examples of fiduciary duties include protecting the clients' privacy, keeping their best interests first, honesty, disclosing all material facts, and reasonable care and diligence.

FIRPTA. FIRPTA stands for the Foreign Investment in Real Property Tax Act of 1980, which imposes income taxes on foreign entities when they sell interest in United States real estate. For example, when a foreign businessman or entrepreneur earns income from a stake held in real property, they are subject to taxation.

First mortgage. A first mortgage is a home loan that claims the primary lien on a property. This is also known as a senior mortgage. For example, when you first purchase your home, the mortgage lender who provided the initial financing would be the first mortgage lender.

First-time homebuyer. An individual who is buying a principal residence for the first time. The purchase doesn't need to be a traditional house for the individual to be qualified as a first-time homebuyer.

Fixity. Fixity means that additions made to the property take a long period of time to pay for themselves and that land can not be moved to a different location. An example of fixity is that a home cannot be moved, and mortgages require several years to pay if full.

Fixture. A fixture is a legal term meaning anything that is attached permanently to real property. An example of a fixture would be a building on the land.

Flat fee listing. Instead of paying a real estate agent a percentage of the sale price, a Flat Fee MLS listing means the client pays a flat rate to have their listing in the Multiple Listing Service. When a Flat Fee MLS is used, the home is technically For Sale By Owner.

Flood insurance. Insurance compensating for the loss by flood damage. It is required by lenders (generally banks) for areas designated with serious flooding potential.

Forbearance. Forbearance is an agreement between the lender and the borrower that will detain a foreclosure. Example: If a homeowner is having financial difficulties but has always paid their mortgage on time, the lender will most likely grant a forbearance, allowing the owner to keep their home.

Foreclosure. Foreclosure is the process or action of a mortgaged property being possessed by the lender due to a failure by the owner to make their payments. For example, when a homeowner misses enough payments, the home goes into foreclosure.

Fraud. Fraud is the act of deception, which results in one party's harm and another party's gain. In real estate, an agent who rents someone a home that is not available for rent is committing an act of fraud.

Freddie Mac. The Federal Home Loan Mortgage Corporation, or Freddie Mac, is another government-sponsored entity. Along with Fannie Mae, Freddie Mac purchases secondary market mortgages and sells them as securities to investors, which increases the money supply for new home purchases.

Functional obsolescence. Functional obsolescence pertains to a property that has features that are neither desirable or practical. For example, a home is 6,000 square feet, but the bedrooms are extremely small.

General contractor. Someone who contracts for the construction of an entire project or building, instead of for a part of the work. He or she hires subcontractors such as electrical contractors, plumbing contractors, etc., coordinates all work, and becomes responsible for payment to the hired subcontractors.

General warranty deed. In real estate, a General Warranty Deed demonstrates and guarantees that a seller has complete ownership of a property. Having a general warranty deed is the safest type of property for buyers to consider.

Gift letter. A written correspondence stating explicitly that the funds received from a relative or a friend are a gift. A gift letter often comes into the picture when a borrower has received financial assistance in making a down payment on a real estate property.

Ginnie Mae. Ginnie Mae is a common term for the Government National Mortgage Association, which is a part of the Department of Housing and Urban Development, or HUD. Ginnie Mae provides better loan prices for mortgage lenders, which allows the lender to offer more loans to its customers.

Good and marketable title. A title that is free from any reasonable doubt. A seller holds an implied obligation to communicate a good and marketable title to the buyer at the date of closing.

Good faith estimate. Also stylized as GFE, a good faith estimate is a document which shows estimates of mortgage payments. Good Faith Estimates allow prospective homebuyers the opportunity to shop with different lenders and compare rates.

Grandfathered in. Typically refers to the legal use of a real estate property depending on the legal existence of the use before a modification of building code or zoning ordinance.

Grant deed. A grant deed is similar to a quitclaim deed and is designed to transfer all interest of ownership from a seller to a buyer. Grant deeds are only utilized in some states, including Texas.

Grantor and grantee. In real estate, a grantor is the current owner of a real estate property, and the grantee is the prospective buyer. Once the transaction is complete, the deed/title is transferred from the grantor to the grantee.

Gross lease. A gross lease is when a tenant pays a flat rental fee, and the landlord or owner pays for the property expenses from that amount. Most apartment and office leases are gross leases.

Ground lease. A ground lease is typically a long-term lease where a piece of land is leased to a tenant who is responsible for all maintenance, taxes, and financing costs. For example, a development company may prefer a ground lease over owning the actual property for an apartment complex.

HELOC. A home equity line of credit, which is often referred to as HELOC, is a loan where the lender agrees to lend a maximum amount and the collateral is in the borrower's home. An example of a HELOC is when the borrower is borrowing against their home to make home improvements in order to increase the value of the home.

Highest and best use. Highest and best use refers to the most probable legal use that produces maximum productivity of vacant land or property. For example, a 10,000-square-foot show floor would be best used as a major retail store.

HOA docs. When someone purchases a property in an HOA, they don't just buy a particular unit. Instead, they purchase into a larger entity that typically holds the ownership of the roof, the clubhouse, etc. HOA docs alert the buyer about building issues like restrictions, building construction quality, etc.

HOA fees. HOA means Homeowners Association, and HOA fees are funds used to cover the costs of services provided to a subdivision. For example, if a subdivision manages the trash disposal, sewer/water, and front yard maintenance, these are covered by the HOA fees.

Hold harmless. It is a statement in a legal contract describing that an organization or individual isn't liable for any damages or injuries to the individual who signs the contract. 'Hold harmless provision' is another term for this clause.

Holdover tenant. If a tenant continues to pay rent after a lease agreement has expired, the tenant is known as a holdover tenant. In the event of a holdover tenant, the landlord can either present a new lease agreement, or consider them a trespasser and initiate eviction procedures. Holdover tenant: A tenant that retains possession after his/her lease has expired.

Home warranties. A home warranty is a contract-specific contract which guarantees the quality and proper functionality of a home's appliances, electrical/plumbing systems, etc. Home warranties, in most cases, will cover the cost of repair should anything stated in the warranty become defective.

Homeowners Protection Act. Also known as the HPA, the Homeowners Protection Act is a law that was created to protect homeowners who no longer need Private Mortgage Insurance. Once a homeowner has acquired enough equity in their home to cover what they owe, the law stipulates that they will no longer have to pay for PMI.

Honest and fair dealing. Also referred to as an Implied Duty of Honest and Fair Dealing, this refers to doing anything that may hurt or injure the other party in a contract, even if it is not in writing. In regard to real estate, when an agent insists on taking a low offer on the home with the intent of speeding up the sale, that is not within the bounds of honest and fair dealing.

Housing expense ratio. A percentage that is derived from dividing all the monthly obligations of a borrower by their gross monthly income. The monthly obligations usually include property taxes, interest, principle on the loan, insurance, etc.

How closing works? The closing date in real estate is usually set weeks in advance and is where the final steps of a real estate transaction are completed. Tasks completed during closing include the transfer of funds from the lender, signing over and transferring the deed, funds are allocated for closing costs, and the final transfer of the deed is completed.

Hypothecation. Hypothecation is a type of collateral offered to secure a loan or other funding, but ownership still remains in control of the borrower. For example, if a homeowner offers their land as hypothecation in order to fund the remodeling of their house, they would still own the land as long as the conditions of the agreement were met.

Immobility. Immobility is anything that cannot be moved; it cannot be moved from one place to another and is affected by the environment around it. An example of immobility is a mall, which cannot be moved.

Implied agency. Implied agency is when an agent gives advice or provides any service without having a formal contract. In regard to real estate, implied agency can occur if a potential buyer asks for your input on a housing price before they sign a buyer's agreement. It is typically a good idea to have a signed agreement in place.

Income approach. Investors use the income approach to estimate the value of a property based on the income it generates. Example: An investor would use the income approach to determine the amount of income generated by a property to estimate how much the property would sell for under current market conditions.

Income property. Property that produces income, generally from rent. It may also include any property which isn't entirely occupied by the owner.

Independent contractor. An independent contractor is a person or business that provides services for a person or business under a verbal or written contract. Independent contractors are different from employees, and real estate agents are an example of independent contractors.

Indestructibility. Indestructibility means that a piece of land cannot be destroyed, even if everything on the land can be. An example of indestructibility is a forest fire. The houses will be destroyed, but the land will still be there, although it will have lost value.

Installment loans. An installment loan is one where a borrower receives a lump sum and makes payments over time. Common examples of installment loans include auto loans and auto title loans.

Installment sales. An installment sale is a property transaction in which at least one payment will be made on the property in the tax year after the transaction was completed. This is also known as the installment method in accounting.

Insurance value. Also called Insurance to Value, this term refers to a type of insurance that accounts for rising costs for repairing or replacing an asset. In real estate, homes generally cost more to repair in the future, so having Insurance to Value will ensure that homeowners are not under-insured.

Interim financing. The process of obtaining short-term, temporary financing to close a real estate transaction. Usually, it is used to cover the remaining purchase price of a second home until the earnings of the first sale are obtained.

Intestate succession. When someone who owns property dies and no will exists, intestate succession is when the state tries to find heirs to their property. In other words, the state will create a will for the deceased when no will currently exists.

Investment value. Investment value is an estimate a company or individual will make based on a variety of factors. In real estate, if a person wants to purchase condos to rent, investment value calculations can help them determine how viable and profitable their investment could be.

Joint ownership. Joint ownership is when two or more people possess equal ownership of a home. For example, when a husband and wife purchase property, they are the most common form of joint ownership.

Joint tenancy. Joint tenancy is a type of property ownership where one or more people own real estate together. In joint tenancy, if an owner dies, their interest is transferred to any survivors without any legal interference.

Judicial foreclosure. A judicial foreclosure is a foreclosure case that goes through the judicial process. In some states, all foreclosures are considered judicial foreclosures.

Jumbo loan. A jumbo loan, or jumbo mortgage, is financing that exceeds FHFA limits. For example, jumbo loans are ineligible to receive guarantees or securitization from Fannie Mae or Freddie Mac.

Junior mortgage. A junior mortgage is any mortgage that is taken after the first mortgage. For example, if a home were foreclosed, and the sale only covered the first mortgage, the first mortgage would be settled and any other mortgages would still be due.

Kickbacks. A kickback is a fee or rebate paid to an agent in favor of receiving business from a vendor or client. In real estate, when a contractor pays a real estate broker to handle any home repair needs for their client's listings, they are receiving a kickback.

Latent defects. In property law, latent defects are issues or problems that would not have been found in a thorough property exam. For example, plumbing that is losing its seal before a sale, but not to the point of leaking until after a sale, is a latent defect.

Lease purchase. Commonly known as rent-to-own, lease purchase is an agreement where tenants may rent a property with the option to buy the house after a specified number of payments. Instead of buying a home, lease purchase contracts allow a tenant to rent a home with the option of buying it later.

Lender's title insurance. Insurance that protects the mortgage lender from any potential lawsuits. Typically, lender's title insurance is required to receive a mortgage loan.

Lessee. A lessee is the formal term to describe a tenant. For example, when a tenant is filling out a lease agreement, they will be referred to in writing as a lessee.

Lessor. In real estate, a lessor is known as a landlord. Lessor is typically the formal term used in contracts.

For example, a rental agreement will refer to a landlord as a lessor.

Leverage. A finance term for the utilization of debt to purchase assets as opposed to cash or other positive equity. In real estate, when an investor borrows cash to buy a multi-unit residential property as a means to turn a profit, that is an example of leverage.

Lien priority. A lien priority is the order in which creditors are paid following a foreclosure. An example of a lien priority would be when a home goes into foreclosure and the owner had more than one debt owed. The lien priority would decide in what order creditors are paid.

Lien theory. In a lien theory state, the borrower holds the deed/title of the home, and the mortgage company places a lien on the title until the home is paid in full. For example, when someone buys a home in a lien theory state, they technically own the home, but the lien from the mortgage company must be satisfied before they can take full ownership.

Life estates. A life estate is when the ownership of land or other property lasts until the owner is deceased. For example, when someone owns a life estate, ownership can be transferred when the owner passes away.

Limited partnerships. A limited partnership involves two or more parties, but with a different structure compared to a general partnership. In a limited partnership, the day-to-day management is handled by the general partner, while the other partners have a limited interest in the company. In regard to real estate, a developer with silent partners who finance the project is an example of a limited partnership.

Lis pendens. In legal terms, lis pendens is a written notice of a filed lawsuit in regard to real estate title ownership. For example, if an heir to property files a claim to a deceased relative's ranch, a lis pendens will be served.

Littoral rights. Littoral rights are related to landowners that have land bordering large lakes and oceans. An example of littoral rights would be a beach-side property next to an ocean; the property owner would have certain rights to the water.

Loan estimate. A form that provides a borrower with important information about the loan, including monthly payment, total closing costs, and estimated interest rate for the loan, among others.

Loan pre-approval. Loan pre-approval is the amount a lender will loan a homebuyer, and the mortgage rates associated with the amount(s). Pre-approval requires a full credit and background check, and dramatically increases their chances of buying a home.

Loan prequalification. Prequalifying for a loan is usually a soft inquiry into a prospective homebuyer's financial and credit history to see if they will qualify for a home loan. Although prequalification is useful, it is not a guarantee of what a buyer will qualify for.

Loan-to-value ratio calculation. LTV ratios are calculated by dividing the value of a property by the total amount borrowed. For example: A $100,000 property with a $20,000 down payment equals $80,000 borrowed. As a ratio, the loan-to-value is 80%, or .8

Loan value. Also known as a loan-to-value ratio, a loan value measures the ratio between how much money is loaned vs the value of the home. For example, a loan-to-value ratio of 50% means that the loan is only half of what the property is now worth.

Lock in rate. The guarantee of a lender to provide a borrower a specific interest rate and loan terms for a certain period of time. It's best to keep the lowest locked in rate possible.

Lot and block. A format of legal land description that is used on plats and maps of recorded subdivided land.

Lot, block, and tract system. The lot, block and tract system is a method used to locate and identify land, in highly populated metropolitan and suburban areas, for lots. It is also referred to as the recorded map or plat system. An example of the lot, block and tract system is used by the US and Canada to divide land into smaller chunks to create communities of homes. loyalty.

Loyalty. It is a fiduciary duty of a real estate agent, and it requires that an agent maintain complete loyalty to their client. For example, if an agent must put the client's best interests before their own.

LTV ratio. LTV ratio means Loan-to-Value ratio, and it is the ratio between the amount borrowed for the home and its assessed value. For example, a $100,000 home, minus a $15,000 down payment, means that $85,000 is borrowed, creating an LTV of .85. The closer the number is to 1, the riskier the loan will be for the lender.

Market cycles. Market cycles are a sequence of events that are reflected in demographic, economic and emotional factors that affect the supply and demand for property. For example, the market typically follows a predictable pattern such as an economic boom followed by a slump which is followed by recovery.

Market value. Market value is a subjective/expert opinion of what a commodity or other saleable good would sell for in a certain market. In real estate, a home's market value is determined by what a buyer is willing to pay for a certain home in a specific area at a certain time.

Marketable title. A marketable title is a title for real property that is free of any litigation or defects, making it one of the safest homes for a buyer to purchase. For example, when a title search is completed, a marketable title is the most desirable outcome.

Master plans. A comprehensive zoning plan for a city, county, or other governmental jurisdiction. A master plan is also utilized by real estate builders for a community or planned subdivision.

Material defects. In real estate, a material defect is an issue with some portion of real property which can affect the value. Examples of material defects include a faulty foundation, damaged roof, or a faulty plumbing system.

Mechanics liens. Mechanic liens are legal documents that reserve contractors or suppliers the right to seek payment not received from the owner of a property. An example of a mechanic lien would be a contractor who was promised payment for work on a property but never received payment.

Megan's Law. Megan's Law is a federal law which requires that all states provide public information regarding the whereabouts of sex offenders. In regard to real estate, most homebuyers will search a database to see how many sex offenders are in a specific neighborhood or city.

Metes and bounds system. The metes and bounds system contains the boundaries of a tract of land that is identified by landmarks. An example of the metes and bounds system is when land is identified by stakes.

Mile, rod, township, section, acre distances. A mile is 5,280 feet, a rod is 16.5 feet, a township is 36 sections, a section is 640 acres, and an acre is 43,560 square feet. Each of these measurements is utilized for survey maps.

Mineral rights. Mineral rights are the rights given to the owner to mine and exploit all minerals on their land. An example of mineral rights would be oil found on the property owners land; they would then have a right to exploit that oil.

Misrepresentations. A misrepresentation is when an agent fails to disclose or misstates a particular issue or defect during a transaction. In real estate, an example of misrepresentation is if an agent knows a home's foundation is faulty, but fails or refuses to disclose this fact to their client.

Mixed use. A kind of urban development that combines residential, commercial, institutional, cultural, or entertainment uses, where those functions are functionally and physically integrated.

Month-to-month tenancy. Also referred to as month-to-month lease, month-to-month tenancy is a lease agreement in which the tenant stays and pays rent on a monthly basis. Short-term rentals and vacation rentals may utilize month-to-month tenants.

Mortgage broker. A mortgage broker is an intermediary between a buyer and a lender who assists the buyer in finding the best terms and loan, and helps in getting the loan to closing.

Mortgage insurance. Insurance that protects the mortgage lender against the losses incurred in the event of a mortgage default, hence enabling the lender to lend a bigger percentage of the sales price.

Multifamily home. Unlike single-family homes, a multifamily home is a dwelling with multiple units, where each such unit has its own bathroom and kitchen.

NAR. NAR stands for the National Association of Realtors, a national trade organization in the United States. The National Association of Realtors features the largest trade network in the country, with the mission of helping the real estate industry thrive.

Necessity. Also known as easements of necessity, this is typically a court-ordered easement by which using a neighbor's land is absolutely necessary. As an example, if a home is landlocked and the only way a property owner or visitor can access a public road is by driving through a neighbor's property, an easement of necessity will be in place.

Negligence. In real estate, negligence is when an agent fails to maintain or execute their contractual duties. For example, if a real estate agent discloses information that is supposed to be confidential, they can be considered liable for negligence.

Net lease. In a net lease, a tenant is required to pay a portion or all of the property taxes, insurance, maintenance, and other associated fees. Net leases are most common in commercial real estate, where the owners do not want to handle the logistics of operating their buildings.

Net listing. A net listing is an agreement that a real estate agent enters into with a seller and that allows the agent to keep the proceeds of a home sale above the fixed amount. These situations are most common when a seller needs to sell their home quickly, and they are only legal in Texas and California.

No doc loans. This term refers to the loans that don't require the borrowers to provide documentation of their personal income to the lenders, or that don't require much personal documentation and are asset-based.

NOI. NOI is the Net Operating Income. It is a calculation that is used to examine the profitability of a real estate investment. Example: The NOI equals the revenue made from a property minus operating expenses.

Non-conforming loans. Non-conforming loans are loans (usually mortgage loans) that do not meet the criteria for conforming loans. Reasons why a loan might be non-conforming include exceeding the conforming loan limit, credit worthiness, or insufficient cash for a down payment.

Non-conforming use. Non-conforming use is when a particular real estate property is used against its zoning intent. Examples of non-conforming use include having a restaurant in one's home or someone living in a commercial office.

Non-exclusive listing. Also known as an open listing, a non-exclusive listing is when a client can list their home with multiple brokers, and the commission is paid to only the broker/agent who finds the actual buyer. These are the most volatile of listing agreements.

Non-judicial foreclosure. A nonjudicial foreclosure is a foreclosure that does not require any involvement of a legal process, which is much faster than a judicial foreclosure. In order for a nonjudicial foreclosure to happen, a deed of trust clause would need to be signed.

Normal wear and tear. Refers to the damage that occurs naturally in an investment property because of aging. Typically, it results from a tenant residing in the property and is considered as normal depreciation.

Notary public. Someone who is authorized by the federal or state government to administer oaths, as well as to attest to the originality of signatures. The authority may be extended by the federal authorization to attest to the originality of certain documents, and to serve as a notary in foreign countries.

Notice of default (NOD). A notification provided to a borrower describing they haven't made their payments by the predetermined deadline, or are in default on that mortgage contract otherwise.

Open listing. An open listing is when a homeowner sells their home on their own. This is also known as a For Sale By Owner or a non-exclusive listing.

Opportunity zones. This refers to economically-distressed communities where new investments, under specific conditions, may be acceptable for preferential tax treatment.

Option contract. An option contract provides a buyer with the exclusive right to purchase a home at a later date for a given price. For example, a buyer can purchase the option for exclusivity to buy a property by a specified date, and no other buyers can be considered.

Oral agreement. An agreement that can create a legally binding, valid contract without the presence of a written document, but there are some exceptions based on the components in the contract and its intended purpose.

Origination fees. An origination fee is a fee paid to a lender, which covers the cost of processing a loan. The origination fee will usually be a fixed amount or a total percentage of the loan amount.

Over-improvement. Improvement that is more extensive compared to what the surrounding neighborhood justifies, or more extensive than what can be economically warranted.

Owner's title insurance. This is insurance that protects the owner and the lender for the owner from any claims made against the home. Although not required, owner's title insurance can come in handy should there be any legal ramifications.

Ownership in severalty. In real estate, ownership in severalty means that property is owned by a single person or entity. For example, if someone buys a home, they have ownership in severalty.

Partition. In real property law, a partition is when two or more landowners cannot agree on the use of land, and an agreement is made to divide the property amongst its owners. This can be a voluntary act, or, if court-ordered, a partition can be mandated in order to settle a real property dispute.

Personal property. Personal property is property that is moveable, unlike a fixture. Examples of personal property are cars and boats.

Pet deposit. An additional security deposit that covers any damage caused by a pet. If damage is caused by a tenant (and it's not due to the pet), landlords usually cannot withhold the pet deposit.

Phishing scams. Typically, fraudulent email messages seeming to come from legitimate sources. Usually, these messages direct the recipient to a spoofed website or get him/her to divulge private information otherwise.

Physical life. Physical life is the time period during which an asset on a property can be expected to remain viable and in existence. Example: A pool has a physical life of approximately 10 years.

PITI. PITI stands for Principal, Interest, Taxes, and Insurance combined into one monthly payment. Taxes and insurance are not typically advertised in home loans, and they can lead to foreclosure if the buyer is not careful.

Planned Unit Development (PUD). A PUD is a community of both residential (single-family residents, condos, or townhomes) and commercial units. PUDs can be either attached or detached units. People often confuse PUDS and condos. The difference is, in a PUD the owner actually owns the land the property sits on; while in townhomes or condos, the property owner does not own land, just the structure.

Plat. A plat is a scale-drawn map of how property is divided within a piece of land. Typically, when you purchase a property you will receive a plat. Examples of plats include lots within a subdivision or a commercial shopping plaza.

PMI. PMI stands for Private Mortgage Insurance, and is typically required when a home is purchased with a conventional loan. Private mortgage insurance protects the lender if the buyer fails to make payments.

Pocket listing. A pocket listing is a practice where a home is for sale, but it is not listed on the MLS, and the agent contacts a small number of agents who may have clients interested in buying. This is utilized when a seller wants to maintain more privacy, and it is a strategy to test the real estate market without going public with the listing.

Points. Also known as mortgage points or discount points, points are fees a homebuyer can pay at closing in exchange for lower interest rates. For example, if a mortgage comes with a 5% interest rate, buying 4 points can reduce your rate approximately one percent.

Power of attorney (POA). A power of attorney in real estate is a legal document that allows someone the authority to buy or sell real estate for a person. An example of POA is when a person, maybe an older parent that lives in assisted living, can't make decisions on their own so they give POA to someone they trust (such as a grown child).

Pre-approval letter. A written commitment from the lender after assessing the ability of a borrower to repay the loan. Before sending a pre-approval letter, lenders may look at employment, income, financial resources, etc.

Predatory lending. Predatory lending involves the unethical practice of coercing or forcing a borrower into unfavorable loan terms. For example, if an applicant is tricked into a loan with extremely high interest rates, they could be the victim of predatory lending.

Prepayment penalty. A clause in a mortgage contract describing that a penalty will be evaluated and imposed if the mortgage is paid off or paid down within a specific period of time. It depends upon a percentage of the remaining mortgage balance or a specific number of months' worth of interest.

Prescription. Also known as adverse possession, an easement of prescription is when someone other than the original owner gains ownership rights on property. An example of easement of prescription is when someone uses someone else's land over a specific period of time.

Prescriptive easements. A prescriptive easement is when someone uses another party's property for a specific period of time without the other party's consent. For example, if someone crosses their neighbor's backyard in order to throw their trash away in the neighborhood dumpster for a set amount of time (depending on the state), this would be a prescriptive easement.

Price-fixing. Price-fixing is the collective agreement for businesses to set/fix prices and fees. In real estate, brokers can not enter into agreements that set their commission or service fees.

Price per square foot. Price per square foot is the calculation of each square foot in the area of a property. For example, if a 1,000-square-foot home costs $200,000, the price per square foot is $200.

Prime rate. In finance, the prime rate is the best interest rate available on the market at a given time. In order to qualify for the prime rate, consumers will typically need the best possible credit scores.

Principal broker. A principal broker is the primary real estate broker who either work independently or manage a team of agents. They are responsible for the actions of all the affiliated agents and brokers within that company.

Principal residence. The main or prime living quarters. It may be declared by the occupant or can be their principal residence based on time spent there. It's important for declarations of homestead and tax purposes.

Principal. A principal is any person involved in a real estate contract. An example of a principal is a seller, buyer or investor.

Principle of a 5 stage life cycle. The principle of 5 stage life cycle is growth, stability, decline, renewal, and revitalization. Example: All neighborhoods have a life cycle and will always be in one of the phases.

Principle of change. The principle of change is knowing that all economic and social forces affect the value of property. Example: If the town is experiencing economic growth, the value of the homes will increase.

Principle of conformity. In real estate, the principle of conformity states that utilizing a real property in a similar manner as the rest of a neighborhood can help protect property value. The principle of conformity is the main reason why homes in specific subdivisions look similar to each other.

Principle of contribution. The principle of contribution (also referred to the principle of marginal contribution) shows that the worth of a property improvement is what contributes to the market value versus what it costs to add the improvement. Example: Having a swimming pool can easily add close to $10,000 to the property value; a pool can easily cost more than $10,000, so the contribution to market value is negated.

Principle of highest and best use. In economics, the highest and best use refers to using a specific service, good, or commodity to its most efficient possible use. In real estate, the principle of highest and best use is utilized by appraisers to determine a property's value. For example, the highest and best use of a commercial building with several offices would be best appraised as a shared office space.

Principle of plottage. Plottage is determined by the increase in value and usefulness when multiple pieces of land are combined. For example, if several small plots designed for stores are combined to create a large office building, the increased value would be referred to as plottage.

Principle of substitution. The principle of substitution is a method used to determine the relative value of a property. Example: If a buyer can purchase a 2500 square foot home with 4 bedrooms and 4 bathrooms, built in 2018 in Arlington, for $350,000, why would they pay $550,000 for a similar house in Arlington?

Principle of supply and demand. The principle of supply and demand is what determines the prices of commodities, goods, and services. In real estate, the combination of supply and demand dictates selling prices. For example, when demand is high and supply is low, the cost of real estate will increase, and vice versa.

Principles of value. There are 3 principles of value: the principle of supply and demand, the principle of highest and best use, and the principle of conformity. Each of these Principles of Value are applicable in commercial and residential real estate.

Pro forma. It describes financial documents developed in advance to demonstrate an expected financial status, transaction, or result.

Probate. Probate is the legal process which takes place after someone dies. Probate court involves ensuring a last will and testament is fully executed, as well as other important tasks, such as final expenses and taxes.

Procuring cause. A procuring cause is utilized as determining who was ultimately responsible for a buyer finding a home, and therefore, who receives the commission. For example, if a buyer is shown a home by two different agents, the procuring cause is used to determine which real estate agent performed the actions that helped the buyer make a decision. These situations are common when a buyer uses one agent, fires them, and buys the same home with a different agent.

Progression. The principle of progression states that lesser-valued assets will increase in value if they are surrounded by higher-valued assets. In real estate, it is common for a homebuyer to purchase the cheapest home in a community, with the hope that its surrounding (higher value) homes will help increase its value.

Promissory note. A promissory note is a written agreement which provides a promise to pay back a loan at a certain interest rate within a set period of time. In real estate, a promissory note can be attached to someone's home as collateral.

Property lien taxes. Property lien taxes are legal claims against a property due to unpaid property taxes. An example of property lien taxes would be a homeowner who has not paid their property taxes; the county or city that is owed taxes imposes a property lien.

Property survey. Property surveys are used to confirm everything regarding a property, including the lot size, boundaries, title search, and deed history. In the home-buying process, mortgage lenders will require a property survey during the closing process.

Property tax calculations. Property taxes are calculated by multiplying the county/state interest rate by the assessed home value. As an example, in Tarrant County, a $200,000 home with a 2.3% tax rate would result in a $4600 tax bill.

Property tax deduction. This refers to local and state property taxes that are usually deductible from federal income taxes. They cover real estate taxes that include any local, state, or foreign taxes, which are imposed for the welfare of the general public.

Property taxes. Property taxes are taxes which are levied on real estate property within a local city or county government. These taxes are typically based on the home's value and are usually included in the mortgage.

Proration. Proration is the allocation of funds which takes place at title closing. For example, if a home takes 3 months to sell, the buyer is responsible for the other 9 months.

Public utility easement. An easement that grants specific rights to the owner of that easement. These easements are expressly dedicated to public utility purposes and are granted upon the actual property purchased by the buyers of subdivided lots.

Puffing. The legal definition of puffing is the exaggeration of certain traits during a transaction. In real estate, an agent who claims that a home has brand new marble flooring when it doesn't is a form a puffing.

Punch list. Matters that require to be rectified in a building or home prior to its sale or acceptance by a new owner. For instance, repairing a leaking water pipe before the property is shown to prospective buyers.

Qualified buyer. A qualified buyer is a prospective buyer that demonstrates the financial and creditworthiness to qualify for a home loan. An example of a qualified buyer is someone who is already pre-approved by a mortgage lender and has plenty of cash reserves to pay a down payment.

Quitclaim deed. A quitclaim deed essentially transfers ownership from a seller to a buyer. For example, when a buyer is taking possession of a home, a quitclaim deed is needed to transfer ownership away from the seller.

R factor / R value. A process to measure the insulating value of heat flow through an object or a material. R value depends on the effectiveness of the insulation.

Radon. Radon is a tasteless, odorless, and colorless flammable chemical element that is also radioactive. One of the best ways to limit the exposure to radon is for homes to be well ventilated, both inside and around the home.

Ratification. In real estate, ratification occurs when a contract has been signed by all parties and is now legally binding. This is when the parties have agreed on all terms of the contract, and any changes or counter offers have been initialed and signed.

Ready, willing, and able. "Ready, willing, and able" is used to describe a potential purchaser who is able to sign a legal contract and purchase a property. Example: A real estate agent wants a "ready, willing, and able" client who is in a financial position to sign with them.

Real Estate Broker. A real estate broker is able to work independently or hire agents for real estate transactions. In order to become a broker, one must work as a real estate agent, take additional education, and pass a state licensing broker exam.

Real Estate Salesperson. Also known as a real estate agent, a real estate salesperson is required to work for a broker in order to represent clients in real estate transactions.

Real property. Real property is any piece of land and anything that is permanently attached to it. An example of real property would be a home or commercial office.

Realtor code of ethics. The realtor code of ethics makes certain that realtors serve the client's best interests. Example: Real estate agents can not mislead clients on savings they can make if they use the agent's services.

Reasonable care. Reasonable care is required by an agent to ensure that the client is protected from foreseeable harm. In real estate, an agent may suggest an expert in structural integrity if a home's roof is suspect.

Rebate. A reduction or discount in the price of an service or product . It is not given in advance but offered back for different reasons.

Recorder of deeds. A government office responsible for maintaining documents and public records, particularly records associated with real estate ownership that offer people, other than a property's owner, real rights over that property.

Recovery fund. Recovery funds are designed to help reimburse anyone who was a victim of monetary damages caused by an agent or broker during a real estate transaction which violates state real estate law. It was created to help victims of misrepresentation and fraud in a real estate transaction. Each state has it's own regulations and policies in regard to their recovery fund.

Rectangular survey system. The rectangular survey system is what the government uses to divide property into defined plots. An example of the rectangular survey system is when townships are created. This system creates a unit of land that is 24 square miles.

Redlining. Redlining is the act of discriminating based on an applicant's location (typically with high default rates) instead of income and creditworthiness. In other words, redlining is the practice of denying entire communities, neighborhoods, or subdivisions access to mortgages and loans.

Referral fee. In real estate, a referral fee is provided to a real estate agent when a client is referred to them in a transaction. For example, if a broker is too busy to follow every lead, they may refer their extra leads to a fellow broker in exchange for a referral fee.

Regulation Z. Regulation Z is a part of the Truth in Lending Act of 1968, and it is designed to protect borrowers and consumers from unscrupulous practices regarding interest rates, policies, etc. As an example, mortgage lenders and credit card companies are required to disclose their policies, late fees, interest rates, and other pertinent information as a part of Regulation Z

Reissue rate. A discount offered by a title insurance company when the earlier policy on the same property was obtained from the same title company.

REITs. A REIT is a Real Estate Investment Trust. These are entities that own income properties and are traded on major stock exchanges. Examples of popular REITs include Vanguard and iShares.

Remainderman. In property law terms, a remainderman is a second-level ownership heir of property in an estate. For example, if a parent leaves their home to their oldest son primarily, and the younger daughter inherits the home if the brother passes away, the daughter is the remainderman.

Rent back. A rent back is when a seller of the home rents from the new buyer after closing, usually due to a delay. As an example, if a seller's new home won't be completed in time, they can opt to pay rent to their new owner and stay while they wait for their new home to be move-in ready.

Rent control. A control on subsidized housing, where the government agency pays a part of the rent, and a maximum amount of rent is established by the agency, not by the landlord.

REO. REO stands for Real Estate Owned, and signifies real property that is owned by a lender when a home isn't sold during foreclosure. When a home fails to sell at foreclosure options, it is considered Real Estate Owned.

Replacement value. Replacement value is determined by how much it would cost to replace a lost, damaged, or stolen good. For example, replacement value insurance would not factor in the market value of a particular good, just its replacement value.

Requirements for a listing agreement. In general, a listing agreement requires a description of the property, a definite termination date, a listing price, a broker's compensation, terms for mediation, and terms for the buyer and seller. In real estate, these are the requirements in order for a listing to be valid.

Requirements for validity (contract). A contract must meet five criteria in order to be valid: consideration (the value exchanged by each party), an offer and acceptance of the specific terms, legal purpose (exchange is not considered illegal), mutual assent (both parties agree to each term), and mentally capable parties. If a contract is missing any of these pieces, the contract is deemed void.

Reserves. The cash accounts kept by an HOA (homeowners association) or condo to cover the future operating expenses. These are funded by HOA dues. Reserves also stand for the cash kept by the lenders in order to pay property taxes and homeowners insurance as payments become due.

Restrictive covenant. A type of agreement that needs the buyer to either abstain from or take a specific action. It is a binding legal obligation written into the deed of a real estate property by the seller. Restrictive covenants can be either complex or simple, and they can impose penalties against the buyers who fail to adhere to them.

Retaliatory eviction. Compelling a tenant to vacate as part of revenge for complaints filed by that tenant against the landlord who fails to maintain the property adequately.

Reverse mortgage. A reverse mortgage is a loan that allows specific homeowners a chance to borrow money against the equity in their home. What makes reverse mortgages unique is that the borrower does not have to make monthly loan payments. In order to be eligible for a reverse mortgage, the borrower must be at least 62 years old, and either own their home outright or have a significant amount of equity in their home.

Reversion. In real estate law, a reversion is when the ownership of a trust or property is reverted or given back to the original trustee. As an example, if the younger daughter is granted ownership, and the older brother is second in line, when the younger daughter passes away, the property is reverted to the older brother.

Revocation. Revocation is a withdrawal of an offer or contract from either party. For example, when a buyer withdraws an offer on a home, it is a revocation.

Right of first refusal. Right of first refusal allows a specific party (or tenant) the right to purchase a property if it is ever offered for sale. A common example of right of first refusal occurs in lease purchase contracts.

Right of survivorship. The right of survivorship is real estate attribute associated with joint ownership, where, should one of the owners die, the other owner automatically takes their share of the home. For example, if a husband and wife own a home, and one of them passes away, if a right of survivorship is in place, the surviving spouse assumes full ownership.

Riparian rights. Riparian water rights is a system that distributes water to those owners that have property in the water's path. An example of riparian water rights would be a resident that owns land that runs into a river and has access to use that section of the river for domestic purposes.

Sales comparison approach. Sales comparison approach is a method that compares a property to other similar properties that have recently been sold. Example: When agents analyze comps for a client, they are using a sales comparison approach.

Salvage value. Salvage value is the value of a commodity or good when it reaches the end of its useful life. A common example of salvage value is cars.

Once a car is no longer driveable, its salvage value is assessed by the value of its parts that are still working.

Scarcity. Scarcity is the inadequate supply of real estate in a particular area sending favorable supply and demand, which results in price increases for the property. An example of scarcity is a seller's market.

Secondary markets. The resale marketplaces of loans where investors and lenders buy and sell existing mortgage-backed securities or mortgages, thereby offering greater availability of funds for the purpose of additional mortgage lending.

Section 8. A program that allows low-income tenants to pay a part of their rent while the balance is paid by the government. In this program, homes and apartments are given on rent by landlords at fair market rates.

Section. A section is an area of land that is measured by one square mile and contains 64 acres. An example of section: This measurement is used to maintain whole numbers of acres.

Seisin. This is an Old English term which states that someone has ownership and title of real property. In real estate, this can also be considered a general warranty deed.

Self dealing. Self dealing refers to the practice of an agent, client, or trustee acting in their own best interests. A common example in real estate is when an agent convinces a client to sell their home at a lower price in order to complete the sale quicker.

Setback requirements. In real estate, setbacks are the distance from which a property must be set back from the front, side, and rear lots of another property. For example, two residential homes in a subdivision may have a setback of 15 feet.

Sheriff's deed. A sheriff's deed is a deed which provides ownership to a buyer at a Sheriff's Sale. Sheriff's sales are held during instances of foreclosure, with the proceeds used typically to settle debts.

Sherman Act of 1890. Sherman Act of 1890 is an antitrust law which prohibits businesses from manipulating markets through monopolization, price fixing, or restricting trade. For example, in real estate, if brokers and agents collude to set their commission percentage at a certain rate, this would be a violation of the Sherman Antitrust Act.

Short sale. A short sale is a home or other property that is sold for less than what is owed by the owner. Short sales are considered better and much cheaper than foreclosures.

Simple interest. Simple interest is calculated by multiplying the principal by the annual percentage rate. The key to simple interest is that it only focuses on a fixed principal. Example: $1,000 in an account at 8 percent interest will result in an $80 gain every year.

Special assessment liens. Special assessment liens are tax liens that are imposed for improvements of a property. An example of a special assessment lien would be if unforeseen disasters occurred and repairs were ordered by an HOA.

Special warranty deed. In a special warranty deed, the seller (grantor) does not guarantee that there are any defects in a warranty outside of their period of ownership. For example, if a seller possessed the home for 5 years, a special warranty deed specifies that they are not liable for any defects found before they owned the home.

Specific performance. When a contract is breached, the harmed party may choose specific performance, which requires that a contract be fulfilled. In real estate, if the buyer breaches the contract, the seller can ask the judge for the buyer to fulfill the contract instead of collecting monetary damages.

Spot zoning. Spot zoning involves placing a small piece of land in a different zone than what it was intended for. The most common example of spot zoning is a neighborhood park in a residential community.

Statute of frauds. The Statute of Frauds requires certain types of contracts to be completed in writing. Examples where the statute of frauds is enforced involve the sale of real estate property.

Statute of limitations. Statute of limitations refers to the maximum amount of time any party can take legal action against another party. For example, a plaintiff may only have 6 years to sue for damages before the Statute of Limitations is enforced.

Steering. In real estate, steering is when a real estate agent guides or 'steers' clients towards or away from a certain neighborhood based on their ethnicity. For example, if a real estate agent shows homes to an African American in a neighborhood primarily occupied by other African Americans, there is a possibility of steering.

Stigmatized properties. A stigmatized property is real property that is ignored by buyers for reasons not involving the conditions of the home. Common examples of reasons include a recent homicide in the home, the neighbors' home, or the neighborhood, or a belief that the home is haunted.

Sub-agent. A sub-agent is an agent who provides real estate services to a buyer, but who is actually representing the seller in a transaction. This form of representation was more common in the 1990s, when many buyers did not have their own representation.

Subdivision. A subdivision is a division of a lot (or any piece of land) into two or more lots (or pieces of land) with the intention of developing and selling the land. An example of a subdivision is a group of tract houses that were developed by the same developer.

Subject to. 'Subject to' refers to a way real estate can be purchased- by the real estate investor taking the title to the property, but the loan stays in the name of the seller.

Sublease. Subleases occur when a tenant leases a property they are renting to another tenant. Subleasing is common when college students move away for the summer, but it may not be allowed in certain lease agreements.

Subprime lending crisis. The subprime lending crisis lasted from 2007 to 2010. A housing bubble caused home values to drop dramatically, and it was a major factor in the Great Recession. Subprime mortgages, which were offered with higher interest rates, are considered by many to have been the catalyst for the housing crisis.

Subprime loan. A subprime loan is a type of loan that is offered to borrowers who do not qualify for a prime rate loan. The specific amount of interest charged on a subprime loan is not set in stone; however, they will always be higher than a prime rate loan. An example of a subprime loan would be when a borrower has been turned down by a traditional lender because of their low credit rating.

Suit to quiet title. A suit to quiet title is a lawsuit which sets to establish ownership of real property. For example, if someone is trying to prove ownership above anyone else, it is a 'quiet' title suit.

Supply and demand. This is a well-known economic pricing model which indicates the relationship of the supply of a commodity and the demand of a commodity. In real estate, the supply of homes for sale in Arlington is lower than the demand, so prices will be higher than they would be if the supply and demand were equal.

Syndicate. Referred to as real estate syndication, this is a form of real estate investing which involves a sponsor and several investors. Similar to crowdfunding, syndication provides an opportunity for investors to buy real estate they may not be able to afford on their own.

Syndication. An aggregation of capital from a group of participants to jointly invest in real estate opportunities. A syndication may be developed to acquire one property or multiple properties.

Tax sale. Public sale of a property at auction conducted by government authority, after a period of time of nonpayment of property taxes.

Tenancy at sufferance. Similar to estates at sufferance, tenancy at sufferance is when a tenant stays in a property past the lease agreement, but before the landlord asks the tenant to leave.

Tenancy at will. Tenancy at will is similar to estates at will, which states that a lease agreement can be terminated and void at any time by either party, given a predetermined notice. Tenancy at will requires the most trust of any lease agreement.

Tenancy by the entirety. A kind of concurrent property ownership that happens when the owners of that property are married to each other at the time of receiving the title. Each spouse holds an undivided and equal interest in the property, together with the right of survivorship, which gives the surviving spouse the legal right to acquire the deceased spouse's share in the property.

Tenancy in common. A non-separated ownership in real estate by multiple persons. The interest need not be equal, and in the case of death of one of the owners, no right of survivorship in other owners exists, unless the will of the deceased person specifies his/her interest in the property be divided amongst the existing owners.

Tertiary market. Refers to a market that offers diversification of market, product, and investment style, which is increasingly becoming the indicator of a robust real estate portfolio, irrespective of its size.

Third-party origination. Refers to the situation where a lender utilizes another party to partially or completely originate, underwrite, process, fund, package, or close the mortgages. The mortgages processed this way are then sold to the secondary mortgage market.

TILA. TILA is an acronym for the Truth In Lending Act of 1968, which was passed as a means to protect consumers from a lack of disclosure on behalf of creditors. For example, if a borrower wishes to apply for a mortgage with an adjustable rate, a creditor must disclose that the payments of these mortgages have the potential to increase.

Time is of the essence. A phrase often used in real estate contracts which means performance by one party within or at the period mentioned in the contract is necessary to enable that particular party to seek performance by the other party.

Title search. A title search occurs after an offer on a home has been accepted, and it involves the research of several sources to find any discrepancies about the home being sold. For example, a title search will include a history of the deed, county records, bankruptcy records, etc.

Title theory. When a home is in a title theory state, the title is held by the mortgage company until the loan is paid in full. In other words, even when someone buys a home, if it's in a title theory state, the lender technically holds the title.

Transfer tax. Transfer tax is a tax levied on the exchange of title from one party to the new owner. Transfer taxes can vary by state or city, and they are also known as excise taxes.

TRID. TRID is the Truth in Lending Act. It is also known as the 'know before you owe' mortgage disclosure rule. Example: TRID was put into place in order to make it easier for buyers to understand the costs they will be facing.

Trust. A trust (or a deed of trust, or trust deed) is when a title is transferred by a property owner (the trustor) to a trustee and is then managed by the latter. An example of a trust is when parents are put in assisted living and need to have their property managed, so they create a trust to allow their children to manage their property.

Uniform Residential Landlord and Tenant Act. Known by its acronym URLTA, it was created in 1972 in order to standardize the rights and responsibilities for both tenants and landlords. There are 6 articles in the URLTA, covering obligations for the tenant and landlord, as well as remedies for both parties.

Unilateral agreement. A unilateral contract or agreement involves only one party having to hold its own end of the bargain. One of the best examples of a unilateral agreement is when a pet owner offers a reward for their lost dog/cat.

Unintentional misrepresentation. A negligent misrepresentation is when someone makes a statement that is not true, without knowing all the facts. In real estate, if an agent claims that a neighborhood is quiet without any knowledge if whether the neighborhood is quiet or not, this could be considered negligent misrepresentation.

Uniqueness. Uniqueness is that land is not uniform; it differs in size, shape and location. An example of uniqueness is two identical houses in the same development with the same build, same lot size and same square footage. They are still in different locations.

Usury lending laws. Usury lending laws stipulate how much interest a lender can charge borrowers. Lending laws are designed to protect consumers from unfavorable interest rates.

VA guaranteed loan. A loan program with which the government offers a guarantee of paying a part of the loan taken by military service members, veterans, and their families. With this guarantee, lenders can offer more favorable terms for VA loans than conventional mortgages.

VA loan. A VA (Veterans Affairs) loan is a mortgage that is guaranteed by the United States Department of Veterans Affairs. The intention of these loans is to supply home financing to eligible veterans and to help veterans purchase properties with no down payment. An example of a VA loan being used is when a veteran has met the eligibility requirements and is considering purchasing a home or refinancing the home they have.

VA. VA stands for the United States Department of Veteran Affairs, a federal agency responsible for the well-being of Veterans. In regard to real estate, the VA offers a housing allowance in their GI Bill.

Variance. In real estate, variance is a written request for landowners to deviate from current zoning laws in regard to their property. This is also known as use variance, and when granted, it allows the zoning requirements to be circumvented for that property only.

Voidable contract. A formal agreement between two parties, which may be rendered unenforceable for different types of legal reasons. Reasons may include fraud or misrepresentation, undue influence, or a mistake, among others.

What does a title attorney do? Real estate attorneys provide a variety of services to ensure that real estate transactions and title transfers are handled properly. Title attorneys will examine purchase agreements, title documents, and more.

What is airspace above the land rights (air rights)? Air rights are the legal right to develop the space above land with no intrusion by others. An example of air rights would be used in New York City where there is not much land left to develop. The city changed their zoning laws, placing restrictions on developers.

Winterizing. The process of preparing a house for cold weather by adding heating units, insulation, etc.

Wraparound mortgage. Wrap-around loans, or wraparound mortgages are junior mortgages which include the current loan on the property, plus an additional loan which covers the price of the property. Wraparound loans are primarily used for refinancing.

Zoning laws. Zoning laws define how specific geographical zones can be utilized within a city, county, or state. These zoning laws can also stipulate other factors, such as building height and lot size. Typical zones can include residential, commercial, administrative, and industrial.

Zoning ordinances. Zoning ordinances are rules and regulations that define how property can be used in their geographic zone. Example: Zoning ordinances are required for sidewalks and bridges.

Made in the USA
Middletown, DE
14 February 2021